COMMONSE

Commonsense Winemaking

by

ANNE PARRACK

Published by
The Amateur Winemakers Publications Ltd.
Andover, Hants.

IBNS 0 900841 52 4

1st EDITION

First Impression May 1978
Second Impression February 1981

Printed in Great Britain by
Standard Press (Andover) Ltd. South Street, Andover, Hants.
Telephone: Andover 2413

Contents

DEDICATION

TO my husband Jim, without whose help in editing and typing of the manuscript this book could never have been produced. His patience, advice and support during my struggles to make good sense of what I wanted to say, have been very much appreciated.

Also to my late mother-in-law, Anna, whose unfortunate incapacity resulted in her living with us—and allowed me the time to write this book.

ACKNOWLEDGEMENTS

MY very grateful thanks to Mrs. Elizabeth Warren who gave her kind permission for me to use her specific gravity table, i.e. Table 1 (pp. 59). To Mr. T. D. Hodkinson, Mr. D. G. Turner, Mr. B. Campbell, Mr. R. Jackson, and Mr. J. Caisley who kindly allowed me to include some of their recipes.

FOREWORD

THE reader may wonder, 'Why another book on winemaking when there are so many others available?' The answer is very simple—the *4 litre (7 pint) method* for preparation of the must, described in this text, is extremely precise and positively ensures that exactly *4.5 litres (1 gallon)* of wine are produced finally with no wastage whatever. The associated use of Table 1 (which is unique) assures the winemaker that the correct alcoholic strength is obtained for each wine type: such precision is lacking in most other books.

In addition, Chapters II, III, and IV contain much information which is not generally to be found in many books on winemaking, and the recipes in the Appendix have *all* been tried and tested.

INTRODUCTION

IN the last twenty years or so, the popularity of amateur winemaking has increased immensely, largely as a result of more and more people developing a taste for wine while on continental holidays. When back home, indulging that taste by buying commercial wines is rather costly, but if one makes one's own, the expense is greatly reduced. Country wines and those made from garden produce may only cost a few pence per bottle! Even if one *buys* produce for winemaking, the cost may still be as little as one fifth of that of the cheaper commercial wines.

Not only is it very cheap, but the quality one can achieve may compare very favourably with some commercial products. Entertaining takes on new dimensions and many new friendships are forged between people sharing the pleasures and interests of the craft.

Apart from these obvious advantages of amateur wine-making, there is the tremendous sense of pride and achievement involved. As a beginner, these feelings are almost indescribable, particularly when tasting that first gallon of crystal clear wine! No other wine made subsequently ever tastes quite as good as that first one!

Some would-be winemakers are a little dubious about the time involved and the space required when one takes up wine-making. These things are rarely a problem. On average, only an hour or two per week are necessary for attending to one's wines and with a little ingenuity, space for storing fermenting and maturing wines may be created quite easily. It is surprising where some winemakers keep their wines!

Equipment is fairly easy to obtain these days and the basic necessities need only cost a few pounds at the outset, being added to later on as and when required.

With the increasing popularity of the craft, many books on the subject have been published. A great deal of confusion is often felt by beginners when trying to assimilate all the information from different books. Many conflicting theories may be found, leaving the beginner not knowing which he or she should follow. Some books are rather over-simplified, not giving sufficient guidance on basic procedures, whereas others are of such a technical and scientific nature that beginners may be put off altogether. It must be stressed that there is no *one way* to make wine—most methods put forward are quite valid, although some are not explicit enough. A number of books also suffer from the fact that the recipes very obviously have not been tried and tested, leading wine-makers to unfortunate failures.

My aim in *this* book is to teach a simple (but comprehensive), logical method in operational sequence, so that it can be followed very easily, even if the winemaker has no scientific knowledge. All the recipes have been carefully formulated and the wines have been critically appraised. Some have been prizewinners in major wine shows. The niche I am attempting to fill is between the over-simplified and the ultra-technical type of book. It is meant to be of help not only to beginners, but to more experienced winemakers also. It is based on my own practical experience and several years of evening class teaching and it attempts to answer the many questions often asked at these sessions.

I sincerely hope that the information in the text will stimulate interest and enthusiasm for this truly absorbing and fascinating hobby and that the 'fruits' of readers' endeavours will be enjoyed for many years to come.

CHAPTER I

EQUIPMENT

NOW that winemaking has become so popular, there is rarely a problem in finding suppliers of equipment. Small shops dealing almost exclusively with wine and beer making products may be found in most towns, while most branches of Boots the Chemists stock their own brand-named goods as well as other makes.

As stated in the introduction, the *basic* necessities may be acquired for the outlay of only a few pounds. More equipment can be bought gradually as the winemaker expands his production over the months and years. The following are the only really essential items that need to be obtained at the outset:

Bucket	1–1½ yds. (metres) Siphon tubing
Demijohns (gallon jars)	Hydrometer and jar
Half gallon jars	Long handled bottle brush
Nylon sieve or straining bag(s)	Long handled wood or plastic spoon
Funnel	Wine bottles
Corks	Labels and capsules
Fermentation locks	Notebook.

These pieces of equipment are dealt with in detail below. In most cases prices are not given, since such information rapidly becomes out of date.

Bucket

This is a vital piece of equipment in which most wines are fermented on the fruit/vegetable/flower pulp for the first few days in order to extract flavour and colour from the main ingredients.

It is preferable to use the pliable or PVC type rather than rigid plastic, since the latter may impart a distinct 'plastic' flavour to the wine. If available, prefer white to coloured buckets, as occasionally colour may be leached from the bucket

Bucket

Demijohn

2·25 litre (½ gall) jar

Nylon sieve

Nylon straining bag

Polythene funnel

a. Bored cork b. Plain cork.
c. Straight bottle cork
d. Flanged bottle cork

Air-lock

Polythene tubing

Hydrometer jar

Hydrometer

Long-handled bottle brush

Fig 1   Basic Equipment

by the acid content of the wine. Yellow should be avoided altogether because of controversy over the potentially toxic cadmium content of the yellow pigment. This having been said as a warning, however, reassurance may be gained from the fact that many winemakers have used yellow buckets over the years without any obvious ill effects.

The ordinary household 2 gallon (9 litre) size is ideal for fermenting single gallons (4.5 litres) of wine plus pulp. Larger buckets which can hold approximately 3 gallons (13.5 litres) will be very useful at times when one wishes to make more than 1 gallon of a particular wine. If the buckets are fitted with lids, it is preferable that these should not be completely air-tight.

Following initial experimentation with a variety of wines, the winemaker may want to restrict his winemaking to a few favoured recipes as his experience grows, but those that he does produce, he may wish to make in 5 or 10 gallon lots (22.5 to 45 litres). In this case a polythene dustbin is ideal, but he should take heed of any warning on an attached label stating that the vessel is *NOT* suitable for brewing!

Old-fashioned glazed pottery vessels are best avoided unless one is sure that they are not *lead* glazed. Poisoning could result if a lead-glazed vessel is used during fermentation.

There are now available quite a number of rather expensive thermostatically controlled fermenting vessels, but one may be pardoned for wondering whether the extra expense is warranted when one can make do quite well with a cheap household bucket or bin.

Gallon Jars or Demijohns (4.5 litres)

Six to twelve jars are useful at the outset, and it must be remembered that a spare, empty jar is required for racking purposes (described in Chapter VI). The initial outlay for these will come to a few pounds, but if treated with care they will give a lifetime of service. Extra jars can be acquired as the winemaker expands his production.

A point worth mentioning here is that 1 gallon (4.5 litres) is equivalent to only six bottles of wine, and six bottles of wine do not go very far! My advice to beginners is to make quite a few more gallons than you think you will require. A good wine will keep well, but it is doubtful if it will be allowed to do so. Friends—not to mention one's own family—get very thirsty!

Demijohns may be acquired from some off-licences (where they have contained cider) or from winemaking suppliers.

Plastic or polythene gallon orange squash containers should be avoided altogether, if possible, because of their thin, rather porous walls through which oxidation can occur and bouquet can be lost, and because it is often difficult to remove the smell of the original contents of the container. If, in desperation, such a vessel is used for fermentation, it should only be for a very short period (2–3 weeks), and the wine should be transferred to a glass jar thereafter. Maturation, which is a long-term process, should never be carried out in these containers.

Since camping has become so popular, there are many different sorts of heavy duty polypropylene or polythene plastic water containers available, some fitted with taps. Such vessels often have quite a strong 'plastic' smell which could ruin a delicate wine, so are best avoided.

The taps in the barrel types of these containers usually have metal screws in them. When in contact with metal, wine can become tainted, hazy and even poisonous due to chemical reaction with the metal. If this type of container is used, the tap should be removed altogether, and replaced by a rubber bung.

Ex-wine fives (5 gallon or 22.5 litre) sherry containers obtainable from off-licences come under the same category as the thin orange squash containers, and should be avoided.

Some winemaking suppliers (mainly the mail-order firms) stock glass fermenting vessels of a greater capacity than one gallon (4.5 litres), which are useful when one wishes to make perhaps a 3 or 5 gallon batch of wine. However these larger jars are difficult to acquire, and most winemakers make do with demijohns.

Glass carboys (as used for indoor gardens) are rather dangerous since they are not constructed to withstand the pressure of fermenting wine, and have been known to burst.

Wine usually spends many months and maybe even years

in the fermenting vessel, at first during the fermentation and then during maturation, and undoubtedly good quality glass is the best choice for the production of good wine. I have not discussed the use of wood casks since few people have suitable storage space for them, nor the expert knowledge required to look after the cask and the wine contained in it. I leave this subject to those who have had experience in this specialised field.

Half Gallon Jars (2.25 litres)

It is most useful to have a good number of half gallon (2.25 litre) jars in which to store clear, maturing wines, leaving the demijohns free for fresh gallons of wine. They may be obtained empty from most off-licences for a reasonable sum, and usually have contained sherry, wine or cider. Of course, one can always buy them full and enjoy the contents until such time as one's own wine is ready for drinking?

It is not really necessary to *buy* half gallon jars, as Winchesters (which are virtually the same size) may be obtained free from chemists. Needless to say, they must be washed thoroughly before use to remove every trace of the chemicals that they have contained.

Nylon Sieve or Nylon Straining Bag(s)

One or other of these items is necessary when straining liquor from the pulp on which it has been fermenting for a few days. A straining bag is to be preferred, since the mesh of a sieve is rather coarse, and too much fine pulp debris may escape through it into the receiving vessel.

My own particular preference is for a coarse mesh bag suspended inside one of finer mesh, an arrangement which speeds up the straining process. A fine mesh bag alone renders the process tediously slow, but if only one bag is to be used it is better than the coarse type, which poses the same problem as the sieve.

Tape loops need to be sewn on to the top of the straining bags so that they can be suspended by some means over a receiving vessel. The winemaker must devise his own suitable method of suspension, but the diagrams Fig. 2 show some

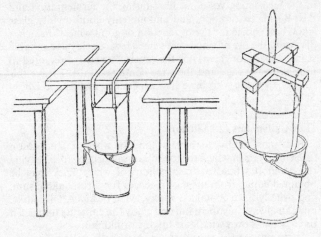

Fig. 2   Methods of Suspension and Straining Bag

possibilities. By alternately raising and releasing opposite pairs of loops, thus agitating the contents of the bag(s), the rate of straining can be considerably accelerated.

The receiving vessel should be either a jar with a large funnel in the neck, or another bucket.

Funnel

The funnel used should be made of plastic or polythene, never of metal, and should have a fairly large diameter (at least 152 mm.). When selecting a funnel for purchase, care must be taken to ensure that the stem will fit securely into the neck of a demijohn. Alternatively, the frame shown in the diagram on page 24 is of very simple construction. Here the platform supports the large funnel over a demijohn containing a smaller funnel, or over a bucket. The straining bags are suspended by strings passing through the tape loops, hanging from nails at the top of the uprights.

A much smaller funnel may be of use for topping up bottles, but this is by no means essential.

Corks

These are required both for jars and for wine bottles. Good quality corks are difficult to obtain, so that it is worth while sorting carefully through loose corks to select the best before making a purchase.

For the standard demijohns and half gallon (2.25 litre) jars, two types of cork are needed. While the wine is fermenting and clearing, a bored cork (see Fig. 9, page 91) fitted with a fermentation lock is necessary, this being replaced by a solid cork when the wine is clear and stable.

A good winemaking supplier will probably have a stock of corks of various sizes which it may be necessary to sort through if the fermenting vessel being used is of other than standard type.

The use of corks, as opposed to rubber bungs, is recommended, since rubber tends to perish after a time, and may stick to the neck of a vessel containing maturing wine. If the wine should unexpectedly start refermenting, the stuck bung will be unable to blow out, and the jar may burst, with unpleasant and possibly dangerous consequences. Additionally bungs are much more difficult to bore to the correct size to accommodate fermentation locks than are corks (though it is possible to obtain them pre-bored to the correct size). They do, however, have the advantage of being impervious to air, thus preventing oxidation which might otherwise occur by passage of air through a poor quality cork.

There are various types of stoppers which may be used for wine bottles. Preferable is the traditional straight-sided cork as used commercially, but there are also flanged cork stoppers, plastic-topped flanged corks and flanged plastic stoppers. The former gives the best seal for long-term storage of wine, but, of course, does have the slight disadvantage in that, once having been removed with a corkscrew it cannot be used again, since bacteria may then gain entry.

The flanged corks are all tapered, and consequently do not give a good seal, especially when bottles are stored on their sides (as they should be). However they are quick to insert, and are very useful for wines that are to be consumed immediately. All-cork flanged stoppers are necessary when exhibiting wines in major shows.

New corks are hard and require softening before they can be inserted in jars and bottles. (The tapered flanged corks are an exception to this general rule, and may only need moistening before insertion in the bottle). Softening corks is best done by soaking them for two hours or so in a mild sulphite solution containing a few drops of glycerine. Corks should not be boiled unless required in a hurry, since such treatment renders them brittle. If they have to be softened rapidly, boil for *one* minute only in a little water containing a few drops of glycerine.

Corking machines may be purchased for the insertion o straight bottle corks, but since these corks can be put in by hand relatively easily, the expense is not essential.

Fermentation Lock (Air-Lock)

Most winemakers consider these simple contraptions indispensable, since they are very effective in keeping flies, beetles, air, dust and bacteria out of fermentation jars, while allowing the carbon dioxide gas evolved during fermentation to escape freely.

These are various sizes and designs available, but the one most commonly used is the small plastic type (Fig. 1). (A larger version can be used with larger fermentation vessels). These are the cheapest to buy (costing only a few pence each) and have the distinct advantage that they are far less fragile than the glass types, and consequently should give many years of service. They can be cleaned quite easily by soaking in hot detergent, and sterilised by immersing in sulphite solution.

The fermentation lock comes into use as soon as the primary fermentation has ceased (usually about 3–5 days after the initial preparation of the must—see Chapter VI). The wine is then in the fermentation jar (having been strained if a pulp fermentation has been conducted) and the jar is fitted with a softened bored cork and fermentation lock. A little stock sulphite solution (see Chapter V, pp. 48) is poured into the air-lock: in the case of the common type shown in Fig, 1, about $\frac{1}{2}''-\frac{3}{4}''$ (13–19 mm.) depth suffices. The dust cap is placed over the central tube to rest in the sulphite solution.

During fermentation, a steady 'blooping' of the air-lock may be heard, occurring in rapid succession during the first few days, but gradually slowing down as fermentation nears completion, thus giving an indication of the rate of fermentation.

It is wise to retain the air-lock in the fermenation jar for a few months after fermentation has ceased. This period during which racking is carried out, allows the wine to clear, almost ensuring that no yeast remains to cause fermentation to recommence, and the air-lock permits the escape of any dissolved carbon dioxide. When the wine is crystal clear and stable, a plain cork bung may be fitted in place of the bored cork and air-lock.

Care should be taken to ensure that the sulphite solution in the air-lock is not allowed completely to evaporate, or spoilage of the wine may occur through entry of air and bacteria. The sulphite should be topped up (if not replaced) every few weeks.

Siphon Tubing

$1\frac{1}{2}$ yds. (metres) of $\frac{1}{4}$ in. (6 mm.) polythene or rubber siphon tubing is required for racking and bottling procedures (see Chapter VI).

Polythene tubing is more convenient than rubber since one can see the flow of wine through it. A strong screw clip to regulate the flow of wine is useful but not entirely necessary. A shallow glass U-tube fitted to the end of the tubing suspended in the fermentation jar will help to avoid the transfer of sediment, but again this is not essential.

Siphon pumps of various kinds may be purchased, the main advantage being that racking is carried out in the absence of air, reducing the chance of oxidising the wine. However if the plain length of tubing is used with care spoilage rarely occurs.

This racking procedure is described in full detail in Chapter VI, and its importance cannot be over-stressed.

Hydrometer and Jar

A hydrometer is a most useful piece of equipment, and

beginners should not be afraid to use one. It is used to estimate the sugar content of juices, to record the progress of the fermentation and to calculate the alcohol content of a finished wine. The scale required reads from 0.990 to 1.170. This instrument and its use are described more fully in Chapter V, pp. 56-63. A tall jar or measuring cylinder is required for use with the hydrometer (see Fig. 7).

Long-handled Bottle Brush

This is a vital piece of equipment for cleaning jars and bottles. The type with a fan of bristles at the end is the most useful.

Long-handled Spoon

A long-handled spoon is necessary for stirring the must during pulp fermentations. Plastic is preferable to wood, as it is more easily kept clean and free from bacteria.

Wine Bottles

These need not be bought, although winemaking suppliers usually stock them. Friends will normally provide sufficient 'empties' for one's needs, but if not, a local restaurant could be a useful source. Do use *wine* bottles, as opposed to whisky or squash bottles. Good presentation can make a good wine seem even better.

Labels and Capsules

Self-adhesive identification labels are very handy for use on demijohns since they may be peeled off and re-applied to other jars when the wine is racked in its maturing stage.

Since all fermenting wines look alike (beige or reddish muddy 'dishwater') it is very wise to use labels for identification on every jar. The type of wine (e.g. apple), the month and the year of preparation are the only pieces of information required. The handypacks of self-adhesive labels which may be obtained from newsagents and stationers are very cheap and last a long time. Tie-on luggage labels are also useful, but less economical.

When bottling wines it is worth taking the trouble to use an attractive label, and finish off the professional effect

Fig. 3 Wine bottle with Label

by fitting a foil or viscose capsule. Bottle labels are available in many designs, and one may print on them the appropriate information regarding each wine (see Fig. 3).

Capsules come in many colours and two main types, as mentioned above. If using foil capsules, a little gadget called a capsuler is a handy implement for ensuring a snug fit around the neck of the bottle. Viscose capsules are supplied in a screw-topped jar filled with liquid which keeps the capsules pliable. When placed over the neck of a wine bottle and left to dry out, they shrink and harden to produce a very good visual effect and an air-tight seal, which is useful if one wishes to store the wine for a long time.

Notebook

Last but not least in this list of necessary items is a note-book of some sort in which to record the recipes, preparation techniques and subsequent management of each wine produced, with relevant dates and quality notes. I find this most useful, since it may be three years or more after preparation before one drinks a wine. It would be impossible to remember exactly what balance of ingredients was used, and how the fermentation progressed. How sad to produce a really good prizewinning wine, and not be able to repeat the experiment through lack of records!

MISCELLANEOUS ITEMS

Juice Extractors and Fruit Presses

These items are very expensive and beyond the means of most winemakers, in addition to being somewhat unnecessary luxuries. Sometimes wine circles possess such pieces of equipment which members may borrow for a small sum. They have the advantage that fruit juices are produced ready for immediate fermentation, thus cutting out pulp fermentations and straining procedures. Wines made from juice so extracted tend to have a better flavour and to mature more quickly than the same type produced by pulp fermentation.

Electric juice extractors are only suitable for fairly firm fruits, since fleshy fruits tend to be reduced to a purée as opposed to the juice being completely separated from the pulp. An old-fashioned jelly bag or a fine mesh nylon straining bag is required to strain the juice produced from *any* fruit, in order to remove small particles of pulp.

Fruit presses may be constructed by the handyman, and there is an excellent book 'Woodwork for Winemakers' by C. J. Dart and D. A. Smith, published by the Amateur Winemaker Publications Ltd., which describes the construction of such an item together with many other useful pieces of equipment for the winemaker.

Steam juice extractors are used by some people, but I am against these in principle because of the 'cooked' flavour imparted to the fruit juice.

Thermostatically Controlled Heaters

Although ideally fermentations should be maintained at constant temperature, thermostatically controlled heaters are something of an extravagance (unless one has an unusually cold house!). Most winemakers manage their fermentations quite well by simply choosing the area of the house that receives the most constant warmth.

If one has a spare cupboard or wardrobe in the home, a handyman can fit it with a light bulb of suitable wattage to create a fairly constant temperature of 60–70°F. (15.5–21°C.) where fermenting wines may conveniently be stored. It is worthwhile insulating the walls of such a fermentation cupboard to prevent undue loss of heat. Polystyrene ceiling tiles are very useful for this purpose.

Thermostats are designed for use with almost any kind of fermenting vessel, and one may also see advertised thermostatically controlled 'hot-plates' which can hold up to two or four demijohns at a time. For those people who brew only a few varieties of wines, but brew in bulk (say 10 gallon—45.5 litres) containers, thermostatic control may become a more realistic proposition, but for most winemakers who may have 5, 10 or even 20 or 30 different wines fermenting actively at any one time, the use of thermostats would be quite out of the question.

Suspension Frame

The accompanying diagram (Fig. 4) gives details of a very easily constructed suspension frame that can be used to support a straining bag and funnel.

The uprights are of 1″ square strip, and the cross-pieces of 1½″ × 1″ strip, butt-jointed, glued and screwed, the central cross-pieces supporting a sheet of 3-ply. The latter has a central hole, the diameter of which depends on the diameter of the funnel that it has to support. It is important to note that the height from the base to the platform will depend on the length and width of the funnel stem above the jar. (The dimensions given are suitable for a funnel of 9″ diameter, used in conjunction with a bucket, or a demijohn in which a smaller funnel is placed). Four screws are part-screwed into the ends of the uprights to serve as catches for the loops of the straining bag which can be suspended over the funnel by the upper part of the frame.

In construction, commence with the centre section so that the sheet of 3-ply screwed to the four cross-pieces can be used to ensure that the frame is squared off.

The whole frame should be primed, given an undercoat and a good coat of gloss. This will facilitate cleaning after use.

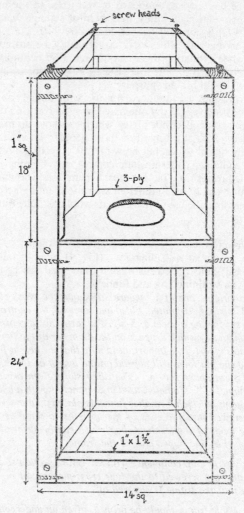

Fig 4 — Suspension Frame

24

CHAPTER II

IN these days when holidays abroad are commonplace most people take wine for granted. We may enjoy many different wines in foreign countries, but how often do we pause to consider what factors are responsible for their characteristics?

It will be of immense help to the amateur winemaker to know just what wine is, and what wine grapes contain that is so vital to the production of good quality wine.

Commercial wine is an alcoholic beverage containing between 8% and 18% alcohol by volume, produced from wine grapes which are crushed and fermented (with or without the skins) under carefully controlled conditions. The end-product is usually a well balanced wine which is typical of the variety of grape used, and the soil and weather conditions under which it is grown. The grapes contain all the essential ingredients that are required for the production of a good wine including enough natural sugar. Only after a very poor season are vintners in some of the more northerly regions of Europe allowed to add a little sugar during fermentation if the grapes have failed to ripen fully.

What, then, does the grape provide?

(1) Flavour, bouquet and body

These qualities determine much of the essential character of the different types of wine, which may vary from the light, delicate Rhine wines to the heavy, full-bodied Sauternes.

(2) Sugar

The amount of sugar present dictates the final alcohol content and the dryness or sweetness of the wine. A grape grown in southern Europe will attain a higher sugar content (due to the hotter, sunnier conditions) than one grown in the northern vineyards of France and Germany.

(3) Nutrients and vitamins

These substances are manufactured naturally by the grape, and are vital to the promotion of a sound fermentation.

(4) Acid

The principal acid found in grapes is tartaric acid, although varying amounts of malic acid are also present. The acidity of a wine is most important since it imparts the 'zest' and 'bite' which interests and stimulates the palate. The level of acidity in commercial wines varies considerably from region to region, the more northerly climes usually producing the more acid wines, such as the German Moselles.

(5) *Tannin*

Tannin is present in the skin of the grape, and occurs in greater concentration in the red than in the white grapes. This accounts for the greater astringency of red wines. Like acid, tannin is vital in small amounts, to provide interest for the palate.

(6) *Yeast*

This is found as the bloom on the skin of the grapes. Each type of grape has its own specific type of yeast, which is in part responsible for the flavour and bouquet of the wine produced.

(7) *Water*

Grapes contain a high percentage of juice, pressed out of them before fermentation, so that in fact no *additional* water is necessary during the production of commercial wines.

(8) *Colour*

White wines can be produced from either white or red grapes, as the juice of the latter is not normally red. After crushing and pressing, the pulp (skins and cell tissue) is removed before fermentation. In the production of red wines, however, fermentation is carried out on the pulp for a few days until sufficient depth of colour has been attained, when the pulp is removed.

It is fairly obvious that most of the flavour ingredients used by amateur winemakers do not contain *all* of the vital attributes mentioned above. Anyone can make 'plonk' by throwing ingredients haphazardly together, and fermenting the flavoured, sugary juice that results, but the quality of the finished product, more often than not, leaves a lot to be desired. The flavour ingredients require to be carefully chosen in order to produce the characteristics of the type of wine that it is desired to make. For example, in the case of flowers, which of themselves only provide bouquet and flavour, it is essential to add dried fruit, bananas or grape concentrate to supply the necessary body, without which the resulting wine would be very unbalanced. Conversely, flower ingredients such as rose petals or wild honeysuckle can be used to enliven the bouquet of otherwise rather dull vegetable wines and some fruit wines.

Sugar is only present in fairly small amounts in most fruits (with the notable exception of dried fruits, which may contain up to 50–60% by weight of sugar), while vegetables and flowers have a negligible sugar content. It is thus essential to add sugar to the must (the mixture of all ingredients that will be fermented to produce the finished wine), and the amount to be added will depend on the estimated sugar content of the ingredients and the desired alcohol content of the finished wine.

Because yeast is a living organism, it requires nutrition and the supply of vitamins if it is to work efficiently to produce alcohol. These have to be added to the must, as few of the ingredients used contain adequate amounts of the necessary foodstuffs or vitamins.

Many of the fruits used in winemaking contain relatively large proportions of acids, whereas flowers and many vegetables contain none at all. Consequently, careful attention has to be paid to ensure the correct acid balance in the wine. In some cases this will require the addition of citric acid (or an 'acid mixture' of tartaric, malic and citric acids), or occasionally excess acid may have to be removed (as outlined in Chapter V).

Tannin is to be found in the skins of all red-skinned fruits, and in apples, pears and gooseberries, etc., but again it is virtually absent from vegetables and flowers. Sultanas, currants and raisins contain significant amounts of tannin, since they are in fact dehydrated grapes. In all cases of deficiency, it will be necessary to add tannin in some form to the must.

Many of the old-fashioned recipes relied for fermentation on wild yeasts present on the fruit or in the air. If fermentation started at all, it was often singularly unsatisfactory, since these yeasts are not necessarily of the type conducive to procuring a good, sound fermentation and high alcohol concentration. In amateur winemaking these wild yeasts are nowadays killed off (or their activity very much reduced) prior to adding a good wine-yeast culture to the must.

Few of the flavour ingredients in general use contain sufficient juice (this will be obvious in the case of flowers), so that the liquid volume will require augmenting with tap water. Pure undiluted fruit or vegetable juices would be too strongly flavoured for most winemaking purposes, as the end result would be more like an alcoholic cordial rather than the subtle flavoured wines that we desire.

Colour is extracted from the ingredients during the initial preparation of the must, or during fermentation on the pulp for a few days. Red wines in particular benefit from pulp fermentation until a sufficiently deep colour has been attained (rarely more than three or four days).

In order to produce a good wine, some thought must go into its formulation and preparation. The next three chapters will clarify and enlarge upon the points briefly mentioned here.

At this point, some would-be winemakers may become discouraged, thinking that it is all too complicated, but this is not so! Admittedly a few basic facts and figures need to be assimilated (these are explained in detail in Chapter V), but after that the whole procedure becomes a logical exercise that can be grasped by anyone. My aim is to enable winemakers to apply commonsense principles to their winemaking, so that they can work out suitable recipes for themselves, rather than rely blindly on recipes of doubtful validity that may be encountered in some of the books currently available. Sample recipes may be found at the end of this book, and should be used as a guide to the balance of ingredients required for the different classes of wines. Once the various principles have been grasped, it should become possible to make a reasonably accurate forecast of the probable outcome of various recipes, and this more critical approach will avoid a lot of wastage and disappointment.

CHAPTER III

WINE may be made by fermenting any sweetened juice, and the characteristic flavours of home-made wines depend on the main ingredient or blend of ingredients used. Commercial wines vary in their flavour and bouquet depending on the type of grape used and the area in which it is grown. In amateur winemaking we use fruit, flowers, leaves, vegetables, dried fruit, grain, grape and other fruit concentrates, either singly or more usually two or three together, to give our wines the characteristics we desire.

There are, in consequence, a multitude of ingredients that may be tried. In this chapter will be found some discussion of the more commonly used 'country' wine ingredients and where to find them, fresh produce available from the garden or the grocers, dried ingredients available either through grocers or from winemaking suppliers, grains, concentrates and other miscellaneous items to be acquired from various sources.

'COUNTRY' WINES

These are the 'old-fashioned' wines that grandmother used to make from wild flowers, leaves and fruit to be found in the countryside. Their popularity has waned somewhat over the years, in some cases, as more sophisticated recipes have been devised, but there is no doubt that many varied and excellent wines can be made from country produce provided that a little care and attention is given to formulating sound recipes.

(1) Flower Wines

These are not over-popular amongst experienced wine-makers, as some believe them to be thin and insipid. In most cases, however, this is due to incorrect formulation, since if made correctly, delightful light table and social wines can be produced. This group forms, in fact, one of my own speci-alities.

The various flower ingredients will be dealt with in the order in which they appear in the countryside. The season given is

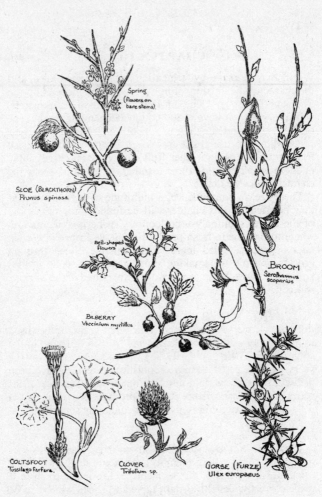

Spring
(flowers on
bare stems)

SLOE (BLACKTHORN)
Prunus spinosa

BROOM
Sarothamnus
scoparius

Bell-shaped
flowers

BILBERRY
Vaccinium myrtillus

COLTSFOOT
Tussilago farfara

CLOVER
Trifolium sp.

GORSE (FURZE)
Ulex europaeus

Fig. 5   Some plants used in winemaking

appropriate for the North of England: in the South, the flowers may appear anything from a fortnight to a month earlier.

Coltsfoot, one of the first colonisers of waste land, is one of the earliest spring flowers, blooming from late February. Dandelions follow from March through to July, and occur in profusion along roadsides and on waste land. Both these flowers are somewhat painstaking to prepare for winemaking, since they should be stripped of all stalk and greenery, to prevent imparting a bitter flavour to the wine.

Gorse is in flower from March to May, and broom during May and June. The former, being intensely spiny, is the more difficult to gather, requiring the use of gloves, and its flavour is, if anything, inferior to that of broom in any event. These two shrubs occur on heathland, hillsides and shrubby verges throughout the British Isles, though the latter is rather local in some areas. They produce a glorious display of brilliant yellow during the spring months.

One minor cautionary note must be sounded in respect of these latter two wines, and this is that a few people appear to be allergic to certain substances extracted from the flowers during the pulp fermentation. Some may even become quite ill (though not seriously, and only for an hour or two) after drinking these wines. I make and drink these wines virtually every year, with no adverse effects to myself or any friends who have chosen to partake. One possible solution is to keep the volume of flowers down to about 3–4 pint measures per gallon (4.5 litres) as a maximum. Recipes in some of the available winemaking books include far too great a volume of flowers.

Hawthorn (May) blossom appears in the hedgerows and on roadsides in May and June, and makes a delightful light wine. The pink variety occasionally occurs, and would give a light rosé wine. The flowers should be stripped from the woody stalks, and any greenery removed.

Clover, in both pink and white forms, flowers from May to September along roadside verges and in meadowland.

Elderflower blooms during June and July, and is common in hedgerows, waste places and old gardens. It is easily recognised by the umbelliferous formation of the flower heads

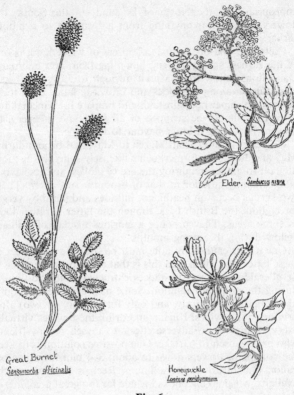

Elder. *Sambucus nigra*

Great Burnet
Sanguisorba officinalis

Honeysuckle
Lonicera periclymenum

Fig. 6

(Fig. 5) and by the angular, hollow stems (used by children for making peashooters). The flowers are small and greenish white, growing in flat-topped clusters at the end of the much branched stems. Some elders are quite small and shrubby, only growing a few feet high, whilst others can grow into quite sizeable trees. There are many different varieties, mostly requiring botanical separation, but for our purposes it is sufficient to note that some varieties have a pronounced 'catty' aroma, and are best avoided if possible. In any event, care should be taken never to use more than ¾ pint (0.43 litres) of these flowers, lightly pressed, since there is a risk of obtaining a distinct aroma of tom-cats even with the milder varieties. Having delivered this warning, it must be said that a well made elderflower wine is one of the most delightful of the country wine group.

Next to appear on the scene is one of my favourites among flower wines, the honeysuckle, which flowers during June and early July with sometimes a second bloom in September. The perfume imparts a beautiful flavour and bouquet to the wine, and thus honeysuckle is very useful in formulating wines of the Sauternes type. We certainly find honeysuckle wine to be the most popular flower wine at our parties. The flowers can be found in tall hedgerows and along the borders of woodland, where the plants climb through the shrubs and young saplings.

Of all the flower wines, however, my prizewinning favourite is that made from burnets (i.e. the Greater Burnet, *Sanguisorba officinalis*). These flower from June to September, and are to be found in damp meadows, by sunny riversides, and in well-overgrown roadside ditches. They reach their northern limit in the British Isles in the Border country, where they are quite scarce, being more widely, but still rather thinly, distributed further south. Though rather difficult to locate. individual colonies once found are usually quite extensivel The plants grow 1½–3 ft. (½–1 m.) tall, and the round to ova, wine-red flower heads occur singly on the end of long, slender sparsely branched stems. The flower head itself is made up of many tightly packed little florets, and might be mistaken, at first glance, for a dead head of knapweed (hardheads) which, however, is dark brown and consists of overlapping scales.

These flowers impart a lovely deep red colour and a pronounced, rich, port-like flavour to the wine.

The flowers mentioned above are those most commonly used for winemaking. Primroses and cowslips have deliberately been omitted in view of the large quantities required and the consequent denudation of the countryside. Cowslips in particular are becoming very scarce in many areas, and are in urgent need of conservation. In any case, it should be standard practice never to completely strip a plant of its flowers—some should always be left to set seed and thus perpetuate the colony.

When gathering flowers for winemaking, a dry, sunny day should be chosen, and the flowers should be completely open, so that the perfume is fully developed. It is wise to confine the flowers in a sealed polythene bag, which both retains the perfume and prevents the escape of insects into the car. Many wild flowers are already beginning to ferment when gathered (due to the presence of natural yeasts in the atmosphere) and these prove very attractive to a wide variety of insects, which rapidly become torpid and often remain on the flower heads after they have been picked. The presence of these insects does not appear to be detrimental to the quality of the wine, so their presence can safely be ignored when preparing the must.

(2) Fruit Wines

Crab apples are probably the earliest of the more popular wild fruits to ripen, and they occur locally along country roads and in tall hedgerows throughout England and Southern Scotland, becoming rather scarcer northwards. The fruit begins to ripen in late summer, and can provide a very pleasant wine provided that steps are taken to reduce the high acidity of the juice. Blackberries (brambles) ripen during August and September, and occur in a variety of forms in hedgerows and the borders of woods throughout the British Isles. Although they do not make a very good wine on their own (imparting only a light red colour and sometimes a slightly 'oxidised' flavour to the wine), when used in conjunction with some other body-giving ingredient(s) (see Chapters IV and V) a very acceptable wine may be produced.

During October and into early November, elderberries become ready for harvesting. When fully ripe, the berries of the commoner species of elder are jet black, and should be hanging head downwards rather than standing upright. The red-stemmed varieties are generally accepted as being the best for flavour. Elderberries are one of the most popular fruits used by winemakers, the wine produced being of an excellent deep red or purple-red hue. They are suitable as a basic ingredient for the production of every type of red wine from a light table wine to a heavy, full-bodied port-type. After a poor summer, the acid and tannin content of the elderberries may be unpalatably high while the wine is still young, but further ageing will usually improve matters. Happily they do not suffer in this way too often!

The sprigs of berries are easy to gather, but removing the berries from the stalks is a long, laborious task, best done by 'strigging' them off with a fork. The end result does make the hard work very worthwhile.

Another fine fruit (for both wine and liqueur making) is the sloe, which ripens during October and November. It is the fruit of the blackthorn, which occurs in scrub, open woodland and hedgerows. The blackthorn is most obvious in March and April when it is covered in white blossom before the leaves appear, and quite a while before the hawthorn flowers. It is a good plan to note down the location of good bushes at this time for future reference, as they are by no means easy to recognise in autumn. Unfortunately, even in a good fruit season, sloes do not set well in the North of England, and the crop is usually very poor. Conditions in the South are usually more favourable, and the crop is appreciably larger.

The fruit is a dull blue-black colour, round or oval, and covered with a pale bloom: in a good season it can grow rather larger than the average blackberry. It does not impart a very deep colour to the wine, but the flavour is delightful.

Sloe gin is an old-fashioned liqueur made by soaking the pricked berries in gin to which has been added the desired amount of sugar: it has a quite superb flavour.

Bilberries (blaeberries in Scotland) are an excellent fruit for winemaking, but are backbreakingly tiresome to collect, since they grow only a few inches high on open moorland or in thin, open woodland developed on acid soil. The berries are small, round and black.

Recipes for hawthornberry and rowanberry wines may be found in many books, but in my own experience these wines usually turn out so bitter that they are not worth making.

'GARDEN' WINES

Anyone who has a garden, no matter how small, should be able to produce some winemaking ingredients. A large garden or an allotment can be a great boon since a variety of fruit trees and bushes, and vegetables may be grown, thereby reducing winemaking costs.

Roses are ever popular, particularly in gardens developed on heavy clay soils, and an excellent wine may be produced from rose-petals, particularly the strongly perfumed varieties of hybrid tea roses. If a high proportion of deep red roses is used, a rosé wine not unlike a Mateus rosé should result. So as not to deprive the garden of its beauty, the flower picking can be delayed until the petals are ready to fall, but before they have withered.

Garden honeysuckle may be used in the same way as the wild form, but it does lack the powerful fragrance of the latter, and the resulting wine is rather disappointing to anyone who has tasted wine made from the wild flowers.

There are a number of other garden flowers, such as pansies, golden rod and wallflowers, that are utilised by some winemakers, but such wines do not have much to recommend them. Herbs such as rosemary and thyme are also possibilities, making interesting wines, but the ingredients require careful control, as the flavour can easily become overpowering, throwing the whole wine out of balance.

Fruit trees and bushes of all kinds will usually provide the winemaker with sufficient fruit both for eating and for winemaking. Apples, pears and gooseberries are very good basic ingredients, and usually do well in the garden. Strawberries, loganberries, raspberries and cultivated blackberries are also suitable, and are relatively easy to grow and look after.

Vines may be grown if one has a greenhouse, but these do require careful treatment, and they take a long time to produce fruit. In recent years, varieties have come on the market that can be grown indoors, but I have little knowledge of the yields that they can give.

Homegrown marrows, carrots, parsnips and beetroot may be used, although in my experience the latter two almost always seem to impart an earthy flavour to the wine. If peas are available, the pods can be used to make a surprisingly good table wine, and this has obvious economic advantages in view of the steadily increasing cost of vegetables. The majority of other common vegetables are not really to be recommended, since the flavours that they confer on a wine are often unacceptable to the palate.

Rhubarb, commonly used by winemakers, suffers from two main disadvantages, the most important of which is its toxic oxalic acid content, which should be removed before fermentation. (Details of the treatment of rhubarb are given in Chapter VI, but it is worth mentioning at this point that the rhubarb sticks should be cut off at least 2 in. (5 cm.) below the leaves, since the main concentration of oxalic acid is found in the leaves). The second disadvantage is that on its own, rhubarb produces a rather thin, insipid wine, and therefore requires the addition of some body-giving ingredient.

WINES FROM COMMERCIAL PRODUCE

Fruit

Fruit is generally considered to be the best basis for winemaking, and, of course, there are always plentiful supplies in the shops. Apples, pears, oranges, grapes and bananas are available all the year round, but are markedly cheaper when in season. Additionally there are many fruits which only have one short season, but can be purchased very economically then. Gooseberries and peaches are two outstanding choices, for the excellent table wines that can be produced from them.

With luck, one may be able to obtain boxes of over-ripe fruit quite cheaply at a weekend. A little time spent in sorting out the best quality produce, discarding any mouldy fruit, will be time well spent. In addition slightly bruised or wrinkled fruit can often be acquired at less than normal prices, and it is a simple matter to cut out any bad areas before use.

Bananas are the more experienced winemakers' 'best

friend', since they can be used in small quantities to add body to any wine without noticeably affecting the flavour. They also greatly assist in promoting the clearing of wines. Black, spotted, over-ripe bananas (which are usually sold off very cheaply by retailers) are the best for use in winemaking. In this state the flavour and sugar content are fully developed and the starch content is reduced. Details of their use are given in Chapters IV and V.

Vegetables

Unlike bananas, vegetables are best bought in peak condition, as otherwise off-flavours can easily develop. In view of present-day prices, this considerably raises the cost of winemaking, with the result that the use of many vegetables is losing popularity. The only really economic proposition perhaps is pea-pod wine, since it has a good flavour, and can be made at no extra cost.

Parsley is a favourite with quite a few winemakers, but requires to be used in conjunction with some body-giving ingredient, since it provides no body on its own.

Tinned and Bottled Fruit Juices

Most tinned fruits will make reasonable wine if used in sufficient quantity—which makes the wines rather expensive to produce. If one has access to a 'Cash & Carry', where catering-size tins may be obtained very much more economically, then using tinned fruit becomes a reasonable proposition.

Tinned or bottled juices are usually more economical, and may even, at times, work out more cheaply than the fresh produce. Orange, grapefruit and pineapple are generally the best buys, and are available in two sizes at most grocers. Bottled apple and grape juice are becoming popular commodities, but they are somewhat more expensive than the citrus juices.

Dried Fruit and Flowers

Currants, raisins, sultanas and dates are readily available in most food shops. Health food stores and winemaking suppliers will usually have stocks of the less readily available figs, apples, apricots and the like. Dried flowers in variety, elderberries, bilberries, rose-hip shells, sloes, bananas and other such dried products normally only used by winemakers, are available from most good winemaking shops or from mail order firms.

OTHER MISCELLANEOUS ITEMS

Jams, jellies and pie fillings are ingredients used by some winemakers, but they are not generally considered too satisfactory, mainly because of their high protein and/or starch content. Grain (rice, wheat, barley and maize) can be obtained from health food and pet shops, and is often used to produce strong wines and sherries.

Grape (both white and red) and many other fruit concentrates are readily available now from winemaking suppliers. These may be used on their own to produce wine of a specific type, or used as additives in smaller quantities in other wines to lend body, flavour and vinosity. Using concentrates on their own is expensive, but the cost can be kept within reason by employing them mainly as additives. A reasonable proportion is, say, $\frac{1}{2}$ pint (284 ml.) of concentrate per gallon (4.5 litres) of wine; one tin of concentrate will then serve 3 gallons (13.6 litres) of wine. As a winemaker gains in experience, he becomes more appreciative of the value of such additives.

This chapter should have given the would-be winemaker some idea of the scope of flavour ingredients that can be used for winemaking. I hope that the section on country wines in particular will stimulate not only the beginner, but also the more experienced winemaker to use the natural, wild ingredients available to him, and to appreciate their worth.

CHAPTER IV

ANY of the fruits, flowers or vegetables already mentioned can be made into dry, medium or sweet wines as one chooses, but experienced winemakers have found, by trial and error, that certain ingredients lend themselves more particularly to the production of specific types of wine, depending on the particular kind of flavour that they impart.

In this chapter, I aim to provide some guide-lines to help eliminate the 'trial and error' stage, so that even beginners will know the ingredients best suited to the type of wine they wish to make. Under each sub-heading, commercial standards are briefly indicated so that one knows what to aim at, and then a selection of suitable ingredients is discussed.

SOCIAL WINES

The majority of home-made wines come under this heading. They are wines intended for drinking socially with friends rather than with a meal, being usually less strong and full bodied than a dessert wine, but having more flavour and sweetness than a table wine. In other words, 'pleasant plonk'.

Their commercial counterparts are fruit wines such as those produced by the Merrydown Wine Co. and one or two other firms. One might buy, for example, a bottle of apricot wine to have on hand in case friends drop in, but one would not dream of serving it with a meal since the flavour would overwhelm the taste of most foods.

In amateur winemaking any ingredient or blend of ingredients may be used and the wine may be made as dry or sweet as one's palate dictates (and to cater for the preferences of one's friends). In all cases, however, it will be necessary to strike a balance between flavour, body, alcohol, acid, tannin and sugar in order to make the wine palatable, and details of how this is done will be found in the next chapter.

Whereas vegetables may not be generally accepted as making good *table* wines, they can be used to produce quite pleasant social wines. Many winemakers put flower wines in the same category, but I beg to differ on that point!

Social wines are usually labelled by ingredients rather than by reference to their use. Experienced winemakers, who like to make wines for specific purposes, or to emulate commercial wines, still tend to produce a fair amount of social 'plonk', so that their quality wines may be preserved for special occasions or competitions.

WHITE DRY TABLE WINES

Commercial wines of this type are usually light to medium bodied, subtle in flavour, with a fragrant, vinous bouquet. They contain 8–12% alcohol by volume, and may vary quite considerably in acid content (as, for example, between the low acidity of the Graves and the quite high acidity of the German Moselles). Some contain a little residual sugar, which takes the edge from their dryness.

These wines are produced to be consumed with food (traditionally mainly with white meat), and they should complement the flavour of the food rather than overpower it.

Gooseberries, apples, peaches, pears, grapefruit or apricots are the main choices of amateur winemakers for this type of wine. The addition of some grape concentrate or sultanas will improve body and vinosity, and enhance the bouquet. Bananas should be avoided or only used in very small quantities as a body-giving ingredient in these light table wines, as their flavour can become rather intrusive.

Flowers may be included to improve the bouquet if desired. Elderflowers (in very small quantity), white and/or yellow rose petals, or honeysuckle are the easiest to obtain and the most fragrant of the flowers for use in this fashion. Dried flowers may be substituted if the fresh ones are not available.

Most winemakers would insist that fruit makes the best table wine, but in my own experience, well made dry flower wines can be superb when served with fish or poultry.

One last point worth mentioning is that a fresher, cleaner flavour is produced in the wine by the use of pure fruit juice than by resorting to a pulp fermentation. This means using a press or electric juice extractor, as already mentioned, which is probably only worth considering for these very light wines.

RED TABLE WINES

Commercial red table wines are invariably very dry, contain 10–12% alcohol by volume, and may be light to medium full bodied, with a fragrant vinous bouquet. The acid and tannin content may vary considerably, but is often high when young, gradually reducing during the long maturation period as they mellow.

The high tannin content of red wines results from the pulp fermentation, during which process it is extracted from the skins, along with the colouring matter.

For the amateur, elderberries, bilberries and blackberries are the choice ingredients for this type of wine. After a good season, the flavour and bouquet provided by these fruits is excellent, but the addition of some body-giving ingredient is usually still required. Blackberries on their own produce a rather thin wine which turns tawny-red in colour after a year or two, and may in the case of some varieties, develop a slightly off-flavour. They benefit from blending with some elderberries or red grape concentrate to provide additional colour, body and flavour.

After a poor season, the acid and tannin content of the fruit may be extremely high, so that fermentation on the pulp should not be prolonged, and the wine may require an extra year or two of maturation before reaching its peak.

Because they are so plentiful, elderberries are the most commonly used fruit for red wine production, although bilberries are superior. Unfortunately the latter are backbreaking to pick, and are expensive to buy, dry or bottled, but the end-product is well worth the additional effort or expense involved.

SAUTERNES TYPE OR WHITE DESSERT WINES

Good Sauternes are a deep golden yellow, very full-bodied, with a powerful, luscious bouquet. They are rich and sweet, and have an alcohol content of 13–17% by volume. They are meant to be consumed with the dessert course of a meal, although they can be drunk with the more strongly flavoured fish (such as salmon), duck or game.

Favourite ingredients for this type of wine include grapefruit, oranges, lime juice, apples, gooseberries, bananas or peaches. If gooseberries or citrus fruits or juices are employed, care must be taken not to use them in too great a concentration due to their high acid content. In the case of apples or peaches, the quantity of fruit should be increased considerably above that required for a dry table wine, to provide the extra body and flavour required.

White grape concentrate, dried fruit (raisins, sultanas or currants) or bananas may be added for body, either individually or as a mixture. Muscatel raisins are particularly useful, since their flavour is very similar to that of the grapes used in Sauternes production. Fresh or dried flowers may be used to enhance the bouquet.

In my own experience, the citrus fruits particularly lend themselves to the production of Sauternes type wines. Particularly in the case of these, but also in other wines of this type, it is advantageous to add 2–3 tablespoonsful of glycerol (glycerine) per gallon. This substance is produced naturally during fermentation to a small extent, but grapes used in the manufacture of Sauternes develop an unusually high glycerol content, which adds to the smoothness of the wine.

SPARKLING WINES

These are not dealt with in this text for two main reasons. In the first place, I have not made such wines myself, and have therefore no first-hand knowledge to impart, and in addition I regard the processes involved to be a little complicated to be undertaken by beginners. To those who wish to know how to produce these wines, I would recommend 'How to make Wines with a Sparkle' by J. Restall and D. Hebbs, published by the Amateur Winemaker Publications Ltd.

PORT TYPE AND RED DESSERT WINES

Red port is better known than white, so I will concentrate on it. It is a sweet, full bodied dessert or after-dinner wine, having a rich, fruity flavour and bouquet, and an alcohol content of 18–20%, obtained by fortification of the original wine.

Elderberries, bilberries, sloes or blackberries are the fruits of choice providing the rich flavour, while body may be supplied by the use of raisins, red grape concentrate, bananas, or a little of all three. Flowers may be added if desired, to improve the bouquet.

The alcohol content should be built up to as high a level as possible during fermentation, and thereafter fortification with a little spirit may be undertaken, though most wine-makers prefer not to do this because of the additional cost involved. With care, it is possible to achieve up to 17% alcohol by natural fermentation, which is quite adequate.

SHERRY TYPE WINES

Commercial sherries are fortified wines that have been oxidised under controlled conditions to obtain their true sherry flavour. It is very difficult for the amateur winemaker to emulate such wines without spoilage occurring from over-oxidation, but with care the result may be very pleasing. In addition, other wines that have begun to oxidise slightly may be converted into passable sherries (provided that they have the correct flavour ingredients) rather than being discarded or used for cooking: slightly oxidised apple wine is a particularly good example.

Detailed instruction in the production of sherries may be found in 'Progressive Winemaking' by P. Duncan and B. Acton, but is again rather beyond the scope of this book, though a rough outline of the management of these wines will be found under the appropriate recipes in the Appendix.

Fino sherries are pale, light bodied and very dry. They contain 16–18% alcohol by volume. Apples, peaches, yellow plums, grapes or sultanas, together with white grape concentrate and/or bananas will provide the light must required for this type of sherry. The fruit flavour should not be too prominent, so that the quantities of fruit should be on a par with those used in table wine production. The required alcohol content can usually be attained by natural fermentation, although fortification may be carried out if desired.

Amontillado sherries are slightly darker, more full bodied and sweeter than finos. The alcohol content is also a little higher, 18–19% by volume. They may be made from similar ingredients, but the amount of body-giving ingredient should be increased. The colour may be deepened by the use of currants or raisins. Fortification may be performed after fermentation if necessary.

Oloroso sherries are rich, dark, full bodied, and contain about 20% of alcohol by volume. These are much easier to simulate than the other types. Raisins, dates, figs and currants, together with plenty of bananas and grape concentrate for body, are the ingredients of choice. Wheat is often used in conjunction with the dried fruit to increase body. Fortification with spirit will usually be necessary to bring the alcohol content up to strength.

APERITIFS

Aperitifs are wines meant to be consumed before a meal, to stimulate the appetite. They usually have a fairly high alcohol content of between 15% and 20%, and may be dry or medium dry. The medium to dry sherries qualify for inclusion in this class, as do the vermouths (which can be prepared by infusing fortified wines with the appropriate vermouth herbs).

Citrus fruits, with their piquancy of flavour, are excellent for the production of aperitifs. The juice plus the strained liquor from an infusion of the finely grated peel are fermented together with some body-giving ingredient (in this case preferably grape concentrate, since it gives a cleaner flavour than bananas or dried fruit, and helps to clear the palate).

Fortification of these various classes, where mentioned, is not absolutely essential, and it does increase the cost of wine production greatly. Most winemakers do not fortify their wines unless preparing a wine especially for a fortified wine class in a show.

LIQUEURS

A true liqueur is a sweetened, flavoured liquor produced by distillation or infusion of herbs or fruit extracts with spirit. The former process is, of course, forbidden by law (except under licence), and heavy fines are imposed on anyone discovered pursuing this pastime.

There is a tremendous variety of liqueurs available commercially, and many of these can be emulated fairly satisfactorily by the amateur winemaker. The requirements are

45

Polish spirit or Vodka as the spirit base, the appropriate liqueur flavouring, sugar syrup, glycerine, and wine of a similar flavour to the liqueur being simulated. These ingredients are mixed together in the approximate proportions indicated in the recipes in the Appendix. The liqueur can be consumed immediately, but usually benefits from a few weeks or months storage to permit the ingredients to blend.

Alternatively, liqueurs may be made by soaking prepared fruit in a Polish spirit, brandy or gin base to which sugar has been added. The mixture is left for a few weeks, and when the fruit is strained off, the liqueur is ready for drinking. If one holidays abroad, spirit may be bought duty-free, thus lowering the cost appreciably.

Liqueurs, though much more expensive to produce than amateur *wines*, are very much cheaper than their commercial counterparts, with which they can compare quite favourably in flavour and general quality.

CHAPTER V

IN this chapter we discuss the facts and figures relating to everything used in winemaking. Broadly speaking, these fall into two categories. Firstly, and very important, information on the cleaning and sterilising of equipment and secondly, details of the basic essentials (mentioned briefly in Chapter II), enabling the winemaker to understand the principles of preparing a well balanced must. A sound understanding of these facts is invaluable if unfortunate, unnecessary mistakes are to be avoided.

(1) EQUIPMENT CLEANSERS AND STERILISING AGENTS

Glassware tends to become badly stained after containing wine for a long time. This is particularly noticeable following red wine production when an unsightly red or brown stain may coat the inside of bottles and jars. Washing with hot detergent rarely removes the stains, but the following three products are very effective:

(a) Domestos

One tablespoon of Domestos in $\frac{1}{2}$ pint (284 ml.) of hot water may be used to rinse out glass containers. If stains are stubborn, the vessels may be filled with a solution of the strength mentioned above and left to soak for about 20 minutes, or longer if necessary. **Thorough rinsing with plenty of water should follow, until no trace of the smell of Domestos remains.**

To ensure that the chemical is completely removed, the vessels may be rinsed out with a little dilute sulphite solution (mentioned below) and then again with water.

(b) Chempro S.D.P.

One to two teaspoonsful of Chempro S.D.P. are dissolved in one gallon (4.5 litres) of warm water and the vessels to be cleaned are filled and left to soak for 20–25 minutes. This should be followed by thorough rinsing with plenty of cold water.

Chempro S.D.P. is caustic and should never be added to wine.

(c) *Silana p.f.*

One level teaspoonful of Silana p.f. crystals are dissolved in ½ pint of hot water and the solution may be used to rinse glassware. Stains are usually removed immediately. If the vessels are very badly stained, a solution of 2 tablespoonsful of the crystals dissolved in one gallon (4.5 litres) of hot water can be tried, leaving the filled container to soak for 20 minutes. This treatment may be repeated if necessary. After using Silana p.f., the vessel should be thoroughly rinsed with water to ensure removal of all trace of the chemical which is caustic and should never be added to wine.

Unfortunately, Silana p.f. tends to leave unsightly white streaks down the sides of glassware so it is preferable to use Domestos or Chempro S.D.P. for wine bottles which are to be used for exhibiting wine. Apart from this one drawback, it is an excellent product.

(2) CAMPDEN TABLETS AND SODIUM METABISULPHITE

Sodium metabisulphite, either crystalline or in the form of the proprietary Campden tablets, is the sterilising agent commonly used in wine production. 'Sulphite' is the term generally used when talking about either the tablets or the crystalline form. The sulphite crystals are much cheaper to buy than the tablets but either can be used, depending on which is more convenient.

When sulphite is in solution, sulphur dioxide gas is released and it is the gas which is the active sterilising agent in the chemical. When concentrated, sulphite has a very pungent odour which 'hits' the back of the nose causing a choking feeling, coughing, and watering eyes. Most yeasts and bacteria are very sensitive to sulphite and are either killed or severely inhibited by its presence. It is most important in preventing oxidation and bacterial spoilage of maturing wines.

(a) *For Sterilising Equipment*

Dissolve *either:* 5 Campden tablets

or   ¼ oz. (7 gm.) sulphite crystals in one pint (568 ml.) of warm water.

Either solution should be stored in a tightly stoppered bottle. It is for rinsing out glassware and all other pieces of equipment used in winemaking. After use the solution may be returned to the storage bottle for future needs. It will keep for many months and is effective as long as the pungent odour remains. After sterilising equipment in this way, rinsing with cold tap water may be carried out.

A little of this solution should be poured into bottles and jars which are not in use. They should be tightly stoppered and will remain bacteria-free until required, when all they will need will be a rinse with cold water.

(b) For Sterilising Musts

One Campden tablet (crushed or whole) per gallon (4.5 litres) is added to the must 24 hours before adding the yeast.

or 5 ml. (one medicinal teaspoonful) of *strong* sulphite solution (see below) is added 24 hours before adding the yeast.

To prepare a strong sulphite solution:

Dissolve 2 oz. (57 gm.) of sulphite crystals in $\frac{1}{2}$ pint (284 ml.) of warm water and make up the volume to *one* pint (568 ml.) with cold water. This solution should be kept in a tightly stoppered bottle and should be used *only* for adding to *wine* and not as a washing solution. This will ensure that it remains uncontaminated.

It is easier and more accurate to use this standard stock solution rather than trying to estimate the correct quantity of the dry crystals. The minute amount required to be added to a gallon (4.5 litres) of wine, is impossible to weigh accurately on household scales and severe and irrevocable 'overdosing' of the must may occur. If this should happen fermentation might never get under way.

N.B. One Campden tablet is equivalent to 5 ml. strong' sulphite solution.

(c) For Preserving Maturing Wines

Add one Campden tablet or 5 ml. of strong sulphite solution per gallon after the first and second rackings to prevent oxidation and bacterial infection. Should fermentation recommence at any time, another tablet or 5 ml. of strong sulphite solution may be added to arrest it.

Should infection occur, double the dose should be added (i.e. two Campden tablets or 10 ml. sulphite).

No more than a total of three tablets or 15 ml. of strong sulphite solution should be used in any one gallon (4.5 litres) of wine, under normal circumstances, otherwise the taste may be impaired. An advantageous side-effect of the use of sulphite is that it promotes glycerol formation during fermentation, adding to the smoothness of a wine at maturity.

(3) FLAVOUR INGREDIENTS

On average, 4 lb. (1.8 kilo) of fruit or vegetables or 4 pints of flowers per gallon (4.5 litres) are required. These quantities, together with some body-giving ingredient, are adequate for most dry table wines and light dry or medium dry social wines. Sweet social and dessert wines, usually predominantly fruit based, can use up to 8 lb. (3.6 kilo) per gallon (4.5 litres). In this case, it is common practice to use a mixture of two or three different fruits so that the flavour of any one does not become overpowering. Mild flavoured fruits, however, such as peaches, pears or eating apples, may be used in these large quantities on their own. More body-giving ingredients are needed in this type of wine and these will also increase flavour, bouquet and vinosity. The concentration of flowers is not normally increased in this fashion in the heavier wines, as the bouquet would become too strongly perfumed and the wine would be unbalanced. Flowers are measured by the *pint*, since they are too light to weigh accurately. They should be placed in a measuring jug and *lightly* pressed down.

Should some of these ingredients have a particularly strong flavour or bouquet, or a high tannin or acid content, it may be necessary to reduce their concentration in the must. Conversely, other ingredients may be required in greater quantities if their flavour or bouquet potential is unusually mild.

The following lists show the more commonly used ingredients and the amount of each required per gallon (4.5 litres), for a basic table wine type or light social wine.

(a) Fruit and Vegetables

    3 lb. (1.4 kilos) Elderberries; blackberries; sloes; bilberries; raspberries; strawberries; crab-apples; cook-

ing-apples; parsnips; citrus fruit; gooseberries; rose hips.

4 lb. (1.8 kilos) Mixed apples; pears; peaches; apricots; plums; damsons; carrots; beetroot; cherries.

5 lb. (2.25 kilos) Marrow; mild flavoured apples; bananas.

(b) Flowers

¾ pint (426 ml.) Elderflower.

3 pints (1.71 litres) Honeysuckle; strongly scented rose-petals.

4 pints (2.3 litres) Coltsfoot; dandelion; gorse; broom; hawthorn blossom; clover; mixed scented and non-scented rose-petals.

5 pints (2.85 litres) Burnets.

6–8 pints (3.4–4.5 litres) Non-scented rose-petals.

These quantities are not varied much since flower wines are usually essentially light in character. Burnets are an exception to the general rule, in that they give rise to a much more full-bodied, port-type wine when suitably complemented with ¼–½ lb. of body-giving ingredient such as raisins. Elderflower, honeysuckle and rose petals *can* be utilised to produce Sauternes-type wines simply by adding more body-giving ingredients (see below—section 4).

(c) Dried Fruit

¾ lb. (340 gm.) Dried elderberries; sloes; rosehips; bilberries; bananas.

1 lb. (0.45 kilo) Raisins; currants; sultanas; dates; figs; apricots; apples.

(d) Dried Flowers

½ oz. (14 gm.) Elderflowers.

1 oz. (28 gm.) Orange blossom; lime flowers.

2 oz. (57 gm.) Rose-petals; dandelions; coltsfoot.

(e) Cereals

1 lb. (0.45 kilo) Rice; wheat; barley; maize.

In the main, winemakers use one basic flavour ingredient together with body-giving ingredients, but a mixture may be used to produce better, more interesting and varied wines. If two or more flavour ingredients are used, the quantities of each should be balanced to add up to the appropriate total for the wine style.

e.g. Blackberry and apple wine—light table wine or light

social wine. Use half the weight of each normally required in one gallon (4.5 litres), that is, 1½ lb. (0.68 kilo) of blackberries and 2 lb. (0.91 kilo) of mixed apples. Any other proportions may be computed as desired.

(4) BODY-GIVING INGREDIENTS

As mentioned in previous chapters, there are three main body-giving ingredients commonly used in winemaking, namely dried fruit (in the form of sultanas, raisins or currants), over-ripe bananas and grape concentrate. Details of the use of each will be found below:

(a) Dried Fruit

¼ lb.–½ lb. (113 gm.–227 gm.) of dried fruit is normally adequate to provide the body required in a light wine. If using Method 1 or 2 for preparation of the must (as described in the next chapter), the fruit should be minced or liquidised and put in with the pulp fermentation. If Method 3, for must preparation is being followed, the dried fruit should be minced or liquidised, reconstituted by cooking in water and the strained juice added to the juice to be fermented, in the demijohn.

The dried fruit may be simmered in 1–2 pints (0.57–1.14 litres) of water in a covered pan for 45 minutes to one hour, or pressure-cooked for 15–20 minutes in 1 pint (0.57 litre) of water at 15 lb. pressure, to obtain the flavoured juice.

(b) Bananas

The best bananas to use are those which are over-ripe and turning black, since at this stage their flavour is fully developed and their starch content reduced. Normally, they may be acquired quite cheaply in this condition.

For light wines, 1 lb. (0.45 kilo) of peeled bananas per gallon (4.5 litres) is adequate. When sweet fuller-bodied wines are required, up to 2 lb. (0.9 kilo) may be used.

In light wines the fruit only should be utilised, the skins being discarded, as they impart too strong a flavour. Even in full-bodied wines, only a few skins should be included.

Bananas, like dried fruit, should be cooked and strained and the 'gravy' added to the must. The fruit is peeled, chopped and simmered for 15–20 minutes in 1–2 pints (0.57–1.14 litres) of water in a covered pan, or pressure-cooked in about 1 pint (0.57 litre) of water for five minutes at 15 lb. pressure. After straining off the liquor the fruit is discarded. The juice obtained is an unappetising grey colour and when left to cool, may turn jelly-like due to the high pectin content of the bananas. (Remember to add a pectin-destroying enzyme).

The addition of banana extract to wines results in increased body and an increased rate of clarification.

If some skins are used, the glycerol content of the wine is raised and this results in added smoothness of the finished product.

Bananas themselves should not be added to pulp fermentations because of their very soft nature when in this over-ripe condition.

(c) *Grape Concentrate*

Grape concentrate is by far the most superior of the body-giving ingredients but it is a little more expensive to use. It provides body, bouquet and vinosity to a wine without adding too much flavour of its own. Wines incorporating grape-concentrate tend to mature more rapidly and have a cleaner taste.

In light social and table wines $\frac{1}{4}$–$\frac{1}{2}$ pint (142–284 ml.) is adequate, whereas in fuller-bodied social and dessert wines, up to 1 pint (568 ml.) per gallon (4.5 litres) is desirable.

Red concentrate is used in red wines only but the white is suitable for red or white wine production.

When a very rich Sauternes or port-type of wine is desired, a little of *all three* of these body-giving ingredients may be used to advantage.

Occasionally, cereals such as rice, wheat or barley are used to provide body. They have some disadvantages in that they impart a rather harsh flavour and the wine tends to take longer to mature than usual. In addition, undesirable starch hazes may result.

If a winemaker wishes to use cereals, $\frac{1}{4}$–$\frac{1}{2}$ lb. (113–227 gm.) per gallon (4.5 litres) is adequate and they should be minced before adding to the must.

(5) BOUQUET IMPROVING INGREDIENTS

All the body-giving ingredients (except cereals) listed above will help to enhance the bouquet of a wine so that there inclusion in the must serves a dual purpose.

In addition, flowers, either fresh or dried, are very useful for improving bouquet. Rose-petals, elderflowers and honeysuckle are the most suitable and they are fairly easily obtained. Half the quantity that would normally be used in a gallon (4.5 litres) of the appropriate flower wine is sufficient. It is very useful to prepare a strong infusion of fresh flowers when they are in season and the strained liquor may then be sulphited and stored in the refrigerator or the deep freeze, ready for use at any time of year. Part of this liquor may be added to wines in calculated quantities.

(6) SUGAR

Sugar is a vital ingredient in winemaking since it is this on which the yeast works during fermentation, converting it into alcohol and carbon dioxide gas.

Any of the common household sugars may be used but the cheapest and most readily obtainable is ordinary granulated sugar. Brown or Demerara sugars are best used only in the production of sherry, port and possibly dessert wines since they impart too much colour and flavour for use in light table wines.

Sugar Syrup

Sugar is most convenient to use in the form of strong sugar syrup (S.S.S.), the latter being:

1 lb. (454 gm.) sugar dissolved in $\frac{1}{2}$ pint (284 ml.) of water to form 1 pint (568 ml.) S.S.S.

$\therefore$ 2 lb. (0.91 kilo) of sugar as S.S.S.$=2$ pints (1.14 litres) S.S.S.

or: 3 lb. (1.36 kilos) of sugar as S.S.S.$=3$ pints (1.7 litres) S.S.S.

The solution is made quite easily by warming and stirring in a pan over heat until all the sugar is dissolved. Do not boil or solid sugar will crystallise out again on cooling. This is the strongest solution of sugar that it is possible to make.

The syrup may be stored for future use if kept in a sterilised, well stoppered bottle in a cool place (preferably in the refrigerator). It should keep free of bacterial infection for quite a few weeks.

There are two important advantages in using strong sugar syrup (S.S.S.) as opposed to solid sugar:

(a) It makes calculating volumes of liquids added to the must very simple. This is important because all three methods used for preparation of the must (described in the next chapter) require the *total* liquid content to be made up to *7 pints* (4 litres).

Example:

A recipe requires that 2 lb. of sugar (0.91 kilo) is to be used.

If 2 lb. (0.91 kilo) sugar is made into S.S.S., 2 pints (1.14 litres) of syrup are obtained. Therefore the volume of the sugar is known accurately and only 5 pints (2.84 litres) of other liquids are required.

(b) If solid sugar is added to a must, a considerable amount of stirring is required to get it completely dissolved. One cannot always be sure that all the sugar has dissolved and if some is left in close contact with the yeast at the bottom of the vessel, the yeast could be killed by the high sugar concentration in that area.

Assessing the Sugar Present in Fruit or Grape Concentrate

It must be remembered when preparing a recipe that many of the flavour and body-giving ingredients contain considerable amounts of natural sugar. This quantity of sugar should be estimated so that the amount of household sugar (in the form of S.S.S.) to be added to the must can be decreased accordingly. Most fresh fruits (except dessert grapes) have a very small sugar content unless used in large quantities, when a few ounces allowance may be made. Dessert grapes have a notably high sugar content so allow approximately $\frac{1}{2}$–$\frac{3}{4}$ lb. (227–340 gm.) of sugar per 5 lb. (2.27 kilos) of grapes.

Dried fruits such as raisins, sultanas, currants, dates, figs and prunes contain approximately $\frac{1}{2}$–$\frac{3}{4}$ lb. (227–340 gm.) of sugar per *pound* of fruit. (454 gm.)

Grape concentrate contains approximately 1 lb. (454 gm.) of sugar per *pint* (568 ml.).

Example:

Suppose a sweet apple wine is required and the main ingredients are: 6 lb. (2.72 kilos) apples

$\frac{1}{2}$ lb. (227 gm.) sultanas

$\frac{1}{2}$ pint (284 ml.) grape concentrate.

The sugar in the apples may be roughly estimated at $\frac{1}{4}$ lb. (113 gm.). $\frac{1}{2}$ lb. (227 gm.) sultanas contain approximately $\frac{1}{4}$ lb. (113 gm.) sugar. $\frac{1}{2}$ pint (284 ml.) grape concentrate contains approximately $\frac{1}{2}$ lb. (227 gm.) sugar.

Therefore, the approximate sugar content of the recipe ingredients is *1 lb.* (454 gm.) which must be subtracted from the amount of sugar required in the original 7 pints (4 litres) of must. From column 2 in Table 1, it can be seen that $2\frac{1}{2}$ lb. (1.13 kilos) of sugar are required in the original must for a sweet wine, therefore only $1\frac{1}{2}$ lb. (680 gm.) of household sugar, in the form of syrup, need to be added.

The Hydrometer

This is a most useful piece of equipment and is basically very simple to use. A typical winemaking (as opposed to beermaking) hydrometer is shown in Fig. 7a) and has a scale reading from 0.990 to 1.170. It is an instrument which measures the specific gravity (S.G.) of a liquid. That is, it compares the density of a liquid with that of water.

S.G. of water $= 1.000$

S.G. of strong sugar syrup $= 1.300$

S.G. of alcohol $= 0.794$

From these figures and the diagram (Fig. 7), it can be seen that a hydrometer will float high up in a 'thick' syrupy liquid and low down in a mixture of water and alcohol.

To obtain the specific gravity (S.G.) of a liquid is very easy. A sample of the liquid is poured into a measuring cylinder or plain hydrometer jar to within 1 in. (25 mm.) of the top. The hydrometer is then lowered gently into the liquid and twirled once or twice to disperse bubbles which might affect the reading. (See Fig. 7b). The reading should be taken at the level of the bottom of the meniscus (see Fig. 7c) of the liquid.

Many beginners are afraid to use a hydrometer, thinking that it is too complicated for them. In fact, it really does not matter whether or not one understands the scientific principles involved—all that is necessary is to be able to read a figure on the hydrometer scale at the level at which it floats in the liquid.

In Fig. 7c it can be seen that the level at which the hydrometer is floating in this particular liquid is 80. This represents

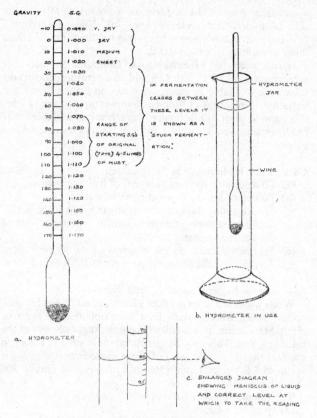

GRAVITY	S.G
-10	0·990
0	1·000
10	1·010
20	1·020
30	1·030
40	1·040
50	1·050
60	1·060
70	1·070
80	1·080
90	1·090
100	1·100
110	1·110
120	1·120
130	1·130
140	1·140
150	1·150
160	1·160
170	1·170

V. DRY
DRY
MEDIUM
SWEET

IF FERMENTATION CEASES BETWEEN THESE LEVELS IT IS KNOWN AS A "STUCK FERMENTATION."

RANGE OF STARTING S.Gs OF ORIGINAL (7 PTS) 4·5 LITRES OF MUST.

HYDROMETER JAR

WINE

a. HYDROMETER

b. HYDROMETER IN USE

c. ENLARGED DIAGRAM SHOWING MENISCUS OF LIQUID AND CORRECT LEVEL AT WHICH TO TAKE THE READING

Fig. 7   The Hydrometer

a *specific gravity* (S.G.) of 1.080, or a *gravity* of 80 (see left side of hydrometer scale in Fig. 7a). The sub-divisions between each major division mean that readings may be taken fairly accurately to within 0.002.

Hydrometers for winemaking are calibrated for use at a temperature of 60°F. (16°C.) and temperature correction tables are available in many winemaking books. Since the variation in readings at different temperatures is very slight, this complication will be ignored here, but it is suggested that readings are taken when the wine is at normal room temperatures.

Uses of the Hydrometer in Winemaking

(a) To determine the sugar content of fruit juices or syrups.

(b) To determine the sugar content of a must.

(c) To determine the quantity of sugar syrup to be added to the must during fermentation, to produce a wine of the desired strength.

(d) To keep a check on the progress of the fermentation.

(e) To calculate the alcoholic strength of the finished wine.

Assessing the Sugar Content of Fruit Juices

When wines are to be produced from tinned or bottled fruit juices, tinned fruit or fresh fruit juice obtained by press or electric extraction, it is useful to know the sugar content of the juice or syrup. This may be calculated quite simply, based on the fact that 1 lb. (454 gm.) of sugar made into strong sugar syrup (S.S.S.) gives 1 pint (568 ml.) of syrup of gravity 300 (S.G. 1.300).

The calculation is as follows:

$$\frac{\text{Gravity of fruit juice}}{\text{Gravity of S.S.S.}} \times \text{Number of pints of juice} = ?\text{lb. sugar}$$

Example:

1¾ pints juice have an S.G. of 1.040 i.e. a *gravity* of *40*

$$\therefore \frac{40}{300} \times \frac{7}{4} = \frac{7}{30} = \text{approx. } \tfrac{1}{4} \text{ lb. sugar.}$$

This weight of sugar is subtracted from the total required in the original 7 pints (4 litres) of must, as described previously.

TABLE 1

1 Wine type	2 Maximum sugar to be included in 7 pints (4 litres) original must	3 Total sugar required in finished gallon (4.5 litres)	4 S.G. If all sugar included in 7 pints original must (4 litres)	5 Required S.G. of finished wine	6 Potential alcohol by volume	7 Comments
Very dry	(0.91 kilos) 2 lb.	(1.02 kilos) 2 lb. 4 oz.	1.097	0.990	11.3%	*Table wines* Extra sugar may be added to
Dry	(0.91 kilo) 2 lb.	(1.19 kilos) 2 lb. 10 oz.	1.114	1.000	13.4%	produce a medium-dry wine if desired
Medium	(1.02 kilos) 2¼ lb.	(1.36 kilos) 3 lb.	1.131	1.010	15.6%	*Social wines*
Sweet	(1.13 kilos) 2½ lb.	(1.53 kilos) 3 lb. 6 oz.	1.148	1.020	17.7%	dessert wines and sweet sherries

See page 60 for example of use of this table.

Use of Table 1

Table 1 shows for each basic wine type, the maximum amount of sugar to be included in the original *7 pints* (4 litres) of must; the *total* sugar required in the finished *gallon* (4.5 litres) of wine, the S.G. one would expect if *all* the sugar were to be included in the original 7 pints (4 litres); the required S.G. of the *finished* wine and the potential alcohol content if *all* the sugar were to be converted into alcohol.

Before preparing a must, decide which type of wine you wish to produce so that you can ascertain from column 2 how much sugar should be included in the original 7 pints (4 litres) of must, to produce a wine of the desired alcohol content and relative sweetness.

It can be seen by comparing columns 2 and 3, that *less* than the *total* sugar required is included in the original 7 pints (4 litres) of must. The reason for this is very simple—yeast cells cannot tolerate a high sugar concentration or they die. No more than 2½ lb. (1.13 kilos) of sugar should be included in the original 7 pints (4 litres) of must for this reason. If, for example, 3 or 3½ lb. (1.36 or 1.60 kilos) of sugar were included in the original must, fermentation probably would commence but would cease prematurely due to death of the yeast cells. The result would be an undrinkable, sickly-sweet wine of poor keeping quality. This state of affairs is described as a 'stuck fermentation'.

For sound fermentation to completion, a starting specific gravity of not more than 1.120 should be obtained. This is an absolute maximum and it is wiser to keep the starting gravity of sweet wines down to approximately 1.110. There will be plenty of space in the demijohn in which to put the extra sugar syrup during fermentation.

When preparing 7 pints (4 litres) of must, the following amounts of sugar should be used (as per column 2, Table 1):

Very dry or dry wine 2 lb. (0.91 kilo)

Medium social wine 2¼ lb. (1.02 kilos)

Sweet social, dessert and sherry type wines 2½ lb. (1.13 kilos)

All *table* wines, which are essentially lower in alcohol than social or dessert wines, should not have more than 2 lb. (0.91 kilo) of sugar included at the outset, so the figures for very dry and dry wines in column 2 are utilised for this type. *After* fermentation, if a medium-dry or medium-sweet table wine is required, a little sugar syrup may be added to raise the S.G. appropriately to somewhere between 1.004 to 1.014 (gravity 4 to 14).

If wished, wines of 8%, 9% or 10% alcohol by volume such as the light German table wines may be prepared by putting in even less sugar than the amount stated for a very dry wine in column 2, Table 1. Such wines should have a starting gravity of between 1.070 (1 lb. 8 oz. or 680 gm. of sugar), and 1.086 (1 lb. 11 oz. or 765 gm. of sugar) in 7 pints (4 litres) and should be fermented to dryness with no sugar additions. A wine containing less than 8% alcohol by volume will have very poor keeping qualities so this should be avoided.

Having ascertained how much sugar (in the form of S.S.S.) to add when preparing the must, all the ingredients are put together as described in the next chapter. The *total* liquid content is made up to 7 pints (4 litres) and the must is mixed thoroughly. A sample of the syrupy must is taken out of the fermentation vessel, strained free of any fruit pulp and poured into the hydrometer jar. A specific gravity (S.G.) reading is taken and noted down with the recipe notes. It is important that this reading is taken *before any fermentation takes place*. The sample of must is returned to the fermentation vessel.

It is now that Table 1 comes into its own. The S.G. reading just obtained will be seen to be less than the appropriate figure in column 4 (which corresponds to the expected S.G. if the *total sugar* required in the *finished gallon* had been put in the *original* 7 pints (4 litres) of must). *Subtract your S.G. reading from the appropriate figure in column 4. The number of points of difference is the number of tablespoonsful of strong sugar syrup to be added to the must in stages during the fermentation.*

Thus the hydrometer is measuring, fairly accurately, the sugar content of the must just prepared and the simple calculation informs the winemaker how much extra sugar is needed to produce a wine of the desired alcoholic strength. Example:

A very dry wine containing approximately 11.3% alcohol is required.

S.G. of 7 pints (4 litres) = 1.080

From column 4 the required S.G. if *all* the sugar had been included = 1.097.

∴ 1.097 − 1.080 = 0.017

∴ 17 tablespoons S.S.S. are to be added to the must in stages.

If this simple procedure is followed for every wine prepared, the winemaker has all the information he needs for producing a wine of the desired alcoholic strength.

Since only 7 pints (4 litres) of must are made up at the outset, it will be obvious that there will be a pint (568 ml.) of space in the demijohn into which the extra sugar syrup can be fed during fermentation.

Adding the Extra Sugar Syrup in Stages

This is generally called 'feeding the yeast'. During the fermentation, S.G. readings are taken every five to seven days. When the reading drops to 1.000 or below, this indicates that the original 2–2½ lb. (0.91–1.13 kilos) of sugar have been converted into alcohol. This may take a few days or a few weeks. It is at this point that the adding of sugar syrup in stages is commenced, at the rate of 5–10 tablespoons at a time, depending on the speed of fermentation. The yeast will now accept this additional sugar. The calculated extra syrup is added in these small doses every time the S.G. drops to 1.000 or below, until the necessary amount has been fed in. At each addition the must should be vigorously agitated to ensure thorough mixing with the syrup.

As fermentation slows down after a few days or weeks, the sugar additions may have to be reduced to only 2 or 3 tablespoons at a time.

When all the extra sugar syrup has been added, the wine may require a little more syrup to raise the S.G. to the required level (see column 5, Table 1). This will apply to medium and sweet wines only, as a rule. The wine should be agitated to ensure thorough mixing of the syrup with the rest of the liquid and should then be left to stand for a day or two to allow the yeast to settle. The wine ought to be racked off the sediment at this stage and the vessel should be topped up with cold tap water. A Campden tablet or 5 ml. of strong sulphite solution is added to inhibit the yeast severely and prevent any further fermentation.

The following two examples will serve to illustrate this procedure of feeding the yeast:

(1) *Very Dry Wine*

S.G. of original 7 pints = 1.085

Using column 4 Table 1: 1.097 − 1.085 = 0.012

∴ 12 tablespoons of S.S.S. are to be added.

2nd reading	S.G. = 1.030	No S.S.S. addition.
3rd reading	S.G. = 0.990	Add 5 tablespoons S.S.S. Mix well.
4th reading	S.G. = 0.990	Add 5 tablespoons S.S.S. Mix well.
5th reading	S.G. = 0.990	Add last 2 tablespoons S.S.S. Mix well.

Allow to ferment to dryness i.e. 0.990.

(2) *Sweet Wine*

S.G. of original 7 pints = 1.110

From column 4, Table 1: 1.148 − 1.110 = 0.038

∴ 38 tablespoons of S.S.S. are to be added.

2nd reading	S.G. = 1.055	No S.S.S. addition.
3rd reading	S.G. = 1.018	No S.S.S. addition.
4th reading	S.G. = 1.000	Add 5 tablespoons S.S.S. Mix well.
5th reading	S.G. = 0.990	Add 5 tablespoons S.S.S. Mix well.
6th reading	S.G. = 0.990	Add 5 tablespoons S.S.S. Mix well.
7th reading	S.G. = 0.994	Add 5 tablespoons S.S.S. Mix well.
8th reading	S.G. = 1.000	Add 5 tablespoons S.S.S. Mix well.
9th reading	S.G. = 1.004	Add 5 tablespoons S.S.S. Mix well.

At this point fermentation has slowed down considerably and the last dose of syrup has not been fermented into alcohol. Thirty tablespoons of S.S.S. have been added, so the extra 8 tablespoons required may now be added to sweeten the wine since no more fermentation is likely to occur due to the inhibitive effect of the high alcohol content of the wine. If the 8 tablespoons of S.S.S. do not add sufficient sweetness, a little more syrup may be added to attain the level desired, usually about S.G. 1.020.

The maximum percentage of alcohol one can hope to achieve is 17–18% since the yeast will not tolerate a higher concentration.

From these two examples, it can be seen that the hydrometer is very useful in recording the progress of the fermentation, and is a good guide as to when to add the extra sugar syrup. It must be stressed however, that the figures given above do not represent a strict pattern to which all wines conform. For many reasons, the fermentation rate may vary and the sugar additions may have to be adjusted accordingly, e.g. add 10 tablespoons of syrup at a time instead of only 5, if fermentation is very rapid.

Some Useful Facts

1 lb. (454 gm.) sugar as S.S.S. = 1 pint (568 ml.) S.S.S.

1 pint (568 ml.) = 40 tablespoons.

1 tablespoon = $\frac{1}{2}$ fl. oz.

1 oz. (28.4 gm.) sugar = $2\frac{1}{2}$ tablespoons S.S.S.

So, every time you add 5 tablespoons of S.S.S. to a wine, you are adding 2 oz. (57 gm.) of sugar.

Assessing the alcohol content of a wine using hydrometer readings is discussed at the end of the next chapter.

(7) ACID

Correct acid balance in a wine is of great importance, giving it zest and bite which interest the palate. Too little acid and a wine tastes flat and uninteresting, too much and it may be completely undrinkable.

In addition to the important effect of acid on the palate, yeast needs an acid medium in which to work effectively. A wine lacking in acid may develop an unpleasant bitter, medicinal flavour due to undesirable chemical reactions taking place in the acid-deficient must during fermentation.

The most common acid used in winemaking is citric, which can either be obtained in crystalline form commercially, or from the juice of lemons.

Citric acid may be bought in bulk from winemaking suppliers much more cheaply than B.P. quality material obtainable from chemists. The crystals are also cheaper and much more convenient than lemons, which vary considerably in size, and therefore in their acid content, as well as being quite expensive.

Citric Acid Requirement per Gallon (4.5 litres)

$\frac{1}{2}$ oz. (14 gm.) in a dry wine
$\frac{5}{8}$ oz. (18 gm.) in a medium wine
$\frac{3}{4}$ oz. (21 gm.) in a sweet wine

Assessing the Acid Content of Fruits

The above figures represent the *total* amount of citric acid required in a gallon (4.5 litres) of wine. Since many of the fruits and body-giving ingredients used in winemaking contain significant quantities of acid, these must be roughly assessed so that the amount of citric acid crystals to be added to the must may be reduced accordingly. There are three main acids which may be found in fresh fruits—citric, malic, and tartaric, and Table 2 (p. 67) shows the principal acid present in most of the more commonly used fruits.

No additional acid will be required when utilising very acid fruits such as citrus fruits; gooseberries; crab-apples; cooking-apples; plums; damsons; apricots; raspberries; strawberries; sloes; blackberries; elderberries; grapes and rhubarb. (Rhubarb may be considered a special case because of its toxic oxalic acid content which many winemakers like to remove before fermentation. As this process removes the other natural acids as well, acid additions must be made as though rhubarb were a non-acid fruit).

Dried fruit such as raisins, sultanas and currants, having originated as grapes, contain a significant amount of acid. For example:

1 lb. (454 gm.) of dried fruit contains sufficient acid for 1 gallon (4.5 litres) of wine.

Therefore, if dried fruit is used in a wine in lesser quantities as a body-giving ingredient, the amount of acid it will supply may be assessed proportionately.

One tin of grape concentrate ($1\frac{1}{2}$ pints or 850 ml.) contains sufficient acid for one gallon (4.5 litres) of wine.

When grape concentrate is used as a body-giving ingredient,

65

the proportion of acid supplied by the concentrate may be assessed, depending on the amount used.

Other fruits, apart from those already mentioned, contain only a little acid, particularly if the fruit is fully ripe when used:

For example, wine made from pears, peaches or bland eating-apples will require almost the full amount of citric acid to be added.

When using tart eating-apples the acid addition may be cut to about $\frac{1}{3}$-$\frac{1}{2}$ of the normal amount.

It is wise to taste the fruit first and try to assess its relative acid content.

This is a rather 'hit and miss' method of assessing the acidity of fruits and the subsequent wines, but the recipes at the end of this book should give some further guidance. For beginners this practice is reasonably accurate and providing that records are kept, valuable lessons may be learned and alterations to recipes can be made for the future, after tasting the final results (i.e. when the wine is *mature*, as very young wine nearly always tastes too acid).

Cereals, vegetables, leaves and flowers contain virtually no acid at all, so that when wine is made from these ingredients the full quota of acid should be added (unless dried fruit or grape concentrate is used in addition for body).

More experienced winemakers tend to prefer to use a mixture of acids rather than citric acid alone. This is mainly because citric acid has a very 'hard' acid taste whereas a mixture of tartaric, malic and citric acids (used in the proportions mentioned below), produces a 'softer' effect on the palate. Malic acid has a more fruity acid taste than the other two. Tartaric, like citric has a very hard acid taste but has the advantage that, during maturation of a wine, some excess is precipitated out as cream of tartar, leaving the wine more palatable.

TABLE 2

Principal Acid Found in Common Fruits

ACID	FRUIT
Citric	Oranges; Lemons; Grapefruit; Pineapples; Strawberries; Raspberries; Pears; Elderberries; Red, White and Black-currants; Bananas.
Malic	Gooseberries; Blackberries; Peaches; Apricots; Cherries; Apples; Loganberries; Damsons; Greengages; Plums; Sloes; Rhubarb (+oxalic acid).
Tartaric	Grapes; Raisins; Sultanas; Currants.

The proportions widely favoured to make up the acid mixture are:

50% tartaric acid; 30% malic acid; 20% citric acid.

These proportions may be altered depending on the principal acid present in the fruit being used, if one wishes. Table 2 (p. 67) shows the main acid constituent of the commonly used fruits.

When using the above acid mixture, slightly more is required than when using citric acid alone because of the 'softer' acid taste of the mixture.

Acid Mixture Requirement per Gallon (4.5 litres)

$\frac{3}{4}$ oz. (21 gm.) in a dry wine

$\frac{7}{8}$ oz. (25 gm.) in a medium wine

1 oz. (28 gm.) in a sweet wine.

Weighing these small quantities presents a problem as household scales are not accurate enough for the purpose. A mini-balance may be purchased from winemaking suppliers and this is very useful though not really a necessity. A simple experiment will enable the winemaker to measure out reasonably accurate amounts of acid without actually weighing them:

Set aside one particular teaspoon which will be used for winemaking purposes. From a bought carton of a known weight of acid (say 4 oz. or 113 gm.) count out how many *level* teaspoonsful of acid are in the container. It will then be easy to calculate how many teaspoonsful are equivalent to $\frac{1}{4}$ oz. (7 gm.) or $\frac{1}{2}$ oz. (14 gm.) etc. This spoon can be used for all acid additions to wines and the accuracy obtained is quite reasonable.

There are some really progressive, scientific winemakers who are at present experimenting with the use of lactic and/or succinic acids in wines. Since simplicity is the purpose of this book, details of the use of these acids will not be discussed here.

Titrating for Acid

As many winemakers become more experienced they want to control the quality of their wines to a greater degree of accuracy.

Titrating for acid in fruit juices and musts is one way of ensuring that the acidity of their wines can be adjusted correctly.

The basic procedure is very simple but beginners (if they are not chemists) tend to be afraid of attempting it because it entails the use of strange equipment and chemicals. They are convinced that they will not be able to understand what they are doing. For such people, the acid-testing kits, which are available from some mail-order winemaking suppliers, provide simple equipment and instructions about its use. The kits use rather small apparatus which unfortunately increases the possibility of inaccurate results but they are cheaper than purchasing the standard apparatus from chemists or laboratory-equipment wholesalers.

The following is a description of the *standard* procedure for titrating for acid:

Standard Apparatus

One 25 ml. burette graduated in 0.1 ml. divisions.

One 10 ml. pipette.

One or two conical flasks.

A burette stand.

Chemical Requirements

$\dfrac{N}{10}$ (decinormal), sodium hydroxide solution.

1 % phenolphthalein indicator solution.

Distilled water (obtainable from chemists or garages).

The sodium hydroxide solution deteriorates if in contact with air so it should be kept in a tightly stoppered bottle.

Method

Rinse out the pipette twice with a little of the wine or must and discard these washings.

Measure out 10 ml. of wine or must with the pipette by sucking the liquid up the tube and placing the index finger over the upper end. Lift the finger fractionally, allowing out a few drops at a time until the liquid is at the 10 ml. level. Transfer the liquid to a conical flask.

Add about 25 ml. of distilled water and a few drops of phenolphthalein indicator to the flask.

Red wines will require greater dilution with distilled water to reduce the intense colour.

Rinse out the burette twice with a little sodium hydroxide solution, then fill it above the zero mark releasing, by the stopcock or tap, a few drops at a time, until the base of the meniscus of the surface of the liquid is at zero (allowing the excess to run to waste). Make sure that there are no air bubbles between the outlet and the stop-cock or tap.

Allow very small quantities of sodium hydroxide solution into the conical flask, swirling the contents continuously and making smaller additions as the end point is approached. When a faint pink colour appears which lasts more than 10 seconds, the end point of the reaction has been reached. Note the volume of sodium hydroxide used from the burette.

Refill the burette and reset at zero. Repeat the titration with another 10 ml. sample of wine as before.

N.B. Wash the burette thoroughly after use to prevent seizing up of the tap due to the presence of alkali.

Take the *average* of the two results obtained, unless the first has obviously overshot the end point by being a much higher figure than the second. In the latter case, the second reading only should be considered.

The acidity of the wine or must is *one half* of this average figure, expressed as parts per thousand (p.p.t.) of sulphuric acid. This is merely a universally accepted standard of measurement and does not mean that sulphuric acid is used in winemaking.

Example:

1st titration used 7.2 ml. sodium hydroxide.

2nd titration used 7.4 ml. sodium hydroxide.

Average $= 7.3$ ml.

$$\therefore \text{Acidity} = \frac{7.3}{2} = 3.65 \text{ p.p.t. sulphuric acid.}$$

If the first titration used 7.6 ml. and the second titration used 7.3 ml., take the latter figure only, since the first probably represents an overshoot.

When titrating a red wine, a greyish colour will be observed in the liquid just before the pink end-point is reached.

A 5 ml. pipette may be used instead of the standard 10 ml. size, in which case the acidity of the liquid is *equal* to the average of the two results. The results obtained when using the smaller pipette are slightly less accurate.

The acid testing kits use a 2 ml. plastic or glass syringe in place of a pipette and burette; 2 ml. of wine or must are titrated with the sodium hydroxide solution. The average result of the two titrations is then *multiplied* by $2\frac{1}{2}$ to give the acidity as p.p.t. sulphuric acid. To make the results more accurate, it is worth trying to obtain a 2 ml. medical syringe of the type used by diabetics. The amount of sodium hydroxide added during the titration can be much more carefully controlled because of the very small outlet of the needle. Consequently, this type of syringe increases the accuracy which is desirable when using such small quantities. A brandy glass in which the liquid can be swirled, is a useful substitute for the test tube which is normally supplied in the kits, since thorough mixing is not easy in a test tube. The brandy glass replaces the standard conical flask.

It must be noted that phenolphthalein indicator solution is sensitive to carbon dioxide. Samples of fermenting musts and very young wines should be boiled for a few minutes to eliminate this gas before they are cooled and used in titrations, otherwise useless, inaccurate results would be obtained.

Acidity Required (expressed as p.p.t. sulphuric acid)

Dry wines   3.0 to 4.0 p.p.t.
Sweet wines 3.5 to 4.5 p.p.t.

These figures are a guide only to the acidity required in wine. A good average level is 3.5 p.p.t.

Greater details about the acidity of the different commercial wines may be found in Duncan and Actons' 'Progressive wine-making' and I would commend this book to anyone attempting to emulate commercial wines.

Important Points to Consider

(a) It is impossible to measure accurately the acid content of a must during the pulp fermentation stage if using Method 1 for preparation of the must (see next chapter). This is because it takes a few days for the acid to be leached out of the fruit into the liquid, so that any measurement of acidity before straining of the must is pointless. Titration should be done on a boiled sample of the must following the straining off of the fruit pulp after three to five days.

(b) When titrating musts for acidity when they are first prepared in the demijohn, or after straining at three to five days, it is important to realise that we have only *7 pints* (4 litres) of must and not a complete *gallon* (4.5 litres) at this stage. In order to calculate what the acidity of the *final gallon* will be, the acidity value obtained (by titration of the sample of the 7 pints (4 litres)) must be *multiplied by $\frac{7}{8}$*. This allows for the final dilution to one gallon (4.5 litres) reducing the acidity. Example:

Acidity of 7 pints (4 litres) of must=4.1 p.p.t.
∴ Acidity of final gallon (4.5 litres)=$4.1 \times \frac{7}{8}$=3.56 p.p.t.

Once the acidity has been calculated, acid may be added to raise the acidity to the required level, or if the sample is over-acid, precipitated chalk or potassium carbonate may be added to reduce it.

To Raise the Acidity

It is useful to know how much acid is required to raise the acidity of a deficient must to the desired level:

⅛ oz. (3.6 gm.) of citric acid or acid mixture will raise the acidity of *one gallon* (4.5 litres) of wine by approximately 0.54 p.p.t.

Example:

Acidity of must (corrected as described above)=3 p.p.t.

Required acidity=3.5 p.p.t.

∴ Add just less than ⅛ oz. (3.6 gm.) of acid to the must to raise the acidity to 3.5 p.p.t.

To Reduce the Acidity

If the acidity of the wine or must is too high, precipitated chalk or potassium carbonate may be used to reduce it:

Precipitated chalk:

¼ oz. (7 gm.) of precipitated chalk will reduce the acidity of 1 gallon (4.5 litres) of wine by approximately *1.5 p.p.t.*

It is not wise to use more than ½ oz. (14 gm.) of chalk for this purpose otherwise it tends to leave behind a rather chalky taste in the wine.

Potassium carbonate:

Potassium carbonate has some advantage over precipitated chalk since it does not leave a chalky taste, but this *may* be replaced by a slightly salty taste in the wine. (The potassium carbonate is more difficult to obtain but mail-order suppliers usually have it on their lists).

Just less than ¼ oz. (i.e. 0.23 oz. or 6.4 gm.) will reduce the acidity of 1 gallon (4.5 litres) of wine or must by 1 p.p.t.

Calculating and Adjusting the Acidity of Juices before Preparation of the Must

When using tinned, bottled, pressed or electrically extracted fruit juices for winemaking, it is worth determining the acidity by titration before making up into 7 pints (4 litres) of must.

The volume of the juice should be measured and the acidity determined. It is then quite simple to calculate what the acidity would be if the juice were diluted to 1 gallon (4.5 litres).

Example:

Two pints (1.14 litres) of juice have an acidity of 16 p.p.t. determined by titration.

When made up to 1 gallon (4.5 litres) of wine finally, the juice will have been diluted to one quarter of what it was originally because the volume has been increased four-fold

∴ The acidity of the final gallon (4.5 litres) will be

$$\frac{16}{4} = 4 \text{ p.p.t.}$$

This figure may be reduced or increased as required, by the methods outlined above.

Any addition of dried fruit or grape concentrate to these juices will increase the acidity. It is advisable therefore to recheck the acidity when the 7 pints (4 litres) of must are in the demijohn.

Use of pH Indicators

It is generally accepted by the more scientific winemakers that obtaining the pH value of a must or wine is of little use in indicating the true acid content of the liquid. The inaccuracy is due to many factors which are far too complicated to discuss here and the practice of using pH indicator papers is rapidly going out of favour.

For those who would like the basic information on the method of obtaining a pH value of their wines and the range required, the following information should suffice.

pH indicator papers with a range from 2.8 to 3.8 should be obtained from laboratory suppliers or possibly winemaking suppliers.

One leaf of indicator paper is dipped into the wine or must and a colour change will be observed. This colour may then be checked against a scale on the cover of the book of papers. When a colour match is found, the pH of the liquid is indicated on the scale.

A wine with a pH of more than 3.5 may be acid-deficient and some acid may need to be added. A wine with a pH of less than 2.9 will be almost certainly over-acid, in which case the excess will have to be removed.

The pH value is not an accurate guide to the acidity of wine. Titrating for acid is the only sure way of obtaining results which are meaningful. Moreover, it is usually difficult to determine the colour of the pH paper with accuracy, and it may be masked (particularly in the case of red wines) by the colour of the wine itself.

(8) TANNIN

The importance of tannin in a wine lies in the astringent quality it imparts. A wine lacking in tannin tastes flat, insipid and uninteresting, whereas an excess of this ingredient results in a harshness which may be totally unacceptable to the palate.

Red wines should contain significantly more tannin than white wines—approximately four times as much.

All the red-skinned fruits contain considerable amounts of tannin, mainly concentrated in their skins. Such fruits include elderberries, blackberries, sloes, bilberries, plums and damsons. In a poor year, when the fruit does not fully ripen, the tannin content of these fruits may be excessive. This applies particularly to elderberries, blackberries and sloes.

Other fruits such as apples (especially crab-apples), pears, gooseberries and grapes also have a fairly high tannin content in their skins.

When making wine from these fruits *no tannin* need be added to the must. When using pears, half the fruit should be peeled and those peelings be discarded before pulp fermentation.

Fermentation on the pulp should be limited to three days when using any of these fruits to prevent the extraction of excessive quantities of tannin.

Dried fruits such as raisins, sultanas or currants (being derived from grapes) contain tannin in their skins. Approximately $\frac{1}{2}$ lb. of these fruits supply sufficient tannin for 1 gallon (4.5 litres) of *white table wine*.

One can (ordinary size—$1\frac{1}{2}$ pints or 850 ml.) of grape concentrate contains the required amount of tannin for 1 gallon (4.5 litres) of the appropriate red or white wine, the red concentrate containing much more tannin than the white as one would expect.

Strangely, oak leaves and burnet flowers are high in tannin

and none need be added to wines made from these ingredients.

Other fruits, vegetables, cereals and flowers contain little or no tannin. All fruit *juices* contain some but the amount is small.

There are various ways in which tannin may be added to a must:

(a) A cup of strong cold tea.

(b) ½ lb. (227 gm.) of dried fruit (i.e. raisins, sultanas, or currants).

(c) Peelings from six average sized pears.

(d) Grape tannin or tannic acid in powder or liquid form.

(a) Adding Tea

This is the old established way of adding tannin to wines and I would think that the great majority of winemakers still use this method.

If dried fruit or grape concentrate are included in the recipe, then the amount of tea added must be reduced accordingly.

One problem with this method is knowing how concentrated to make the tea, which is very difficult to reproduce consistently. With the advent of tea-bags, the problem has eased somewhat—a cup of tea made with *one tea-bag* should provide about the right amount of tannin for 1 gallon (4.5 litres) of wine.

(b) Adding Dried Fruit

In many wines (flower wines in particular), dried fruit is often used to provide body and vinosity. It will also provide tannin and if ½ lb. (227 gm.) of dried fruit per gallon (4.5 litres) is used, the tannin content will be adequate.

Note that if grape concentrate is included in addition to dried fruit, extra tannin is obtained from the concentrate. Care must be taken not to utilise too much of these ingredients in very light wines or the tannin content of the wine may be too high, thus making the wine unbalanced.

(c) Adding Pear Peelings

This method of adding tannin is rather inconvenient and expensive unless one happens to have a pear tree in the garden. Even then the pears would only be available for a short season. Altogether, this is an impracticable way of providing tannin. Having said this, if pears are available, the peelings of *six* average sized fruits are usually adequate for 1 gallon (4.5 litres) of wine, and should be included in the pulp fermentation.

(*d*) *Adding Grape Tannin or Tannic Acid*

Using either of these substances is the best way to regulate the tannin additions to a must.

They may be bought in powder or liquid form and directions for use are usually printed clearly on the container label.

(i) Powder Form

Only 1/15–1/12 oz. (1.9–2.4 gm.) of either grape tannin or tannic acid are required in 1 gallon (4.5 litres) when the must has little or no natural tannin in it. These quantities are too minute to weigh accurately so the powder should be made up into a standard stock solution from which measured amounts may be used.

Standard solution:

Dissolve ½ oz. (14 gm.) of either powder in ¾ pint (426 ml.) of boiled water.

1 fl. oz. of this solution contains 1/30 oz. (0.95 gm.) of tannin.

1 fl. oz. = 2 tablespoonsful

∴ 1 tablespoonful of this solution contains 1/60 oz. (0.47 gm.) of tannin.

To fruit wines in which there will be *a little* natural tannin from the fruit juice, *4 tablespoonsful* (i.e. 1/15 oz. or 1.9 gm. of tannin) of this solution should be added.

To musts containing *no* natural tannin add *5 tablespoonsful* (1/12 oz. or 2.4 gm. of tannin).

This method allows small amounts of tannin to be added to the must with quite reasonable accuracy.

The amount of tannin to be added to the must may be adjusted when dried fruit or grape concentrate is to be included in the recipe.

With a few sulphite crystals added to prevent mould formation, the solution may be kept for quite a few weeks in a tightly stoppered bottle. The bottle should be shaken well before using the solution since some of the tannin tends to settle out on the bottom of the bottle.

(ii) Liquid Form

A number of manufacturers supply 'wine tannin' in liquid form—usually a very concentrated solution of tannin in alcohol. Only a *few drops* of such a solution are required per gallon (4.5 litres) of wine and care should be taken to read the manufacturers' instructions thoroughly before use. The concentration of such a solution may vary between the different manufacturers so that no guide as to the amount to be used can be given here.

Testing for Tannin

Unfortunately, testing for the tannin content of wines or musts can only be done using laboratory facilities. The amateur winemaker has to make do with estimations as described above. Experience teaches one a great deal.

(9) YEAST

When yeast is introduced into an acidic, sweetened juice, it acts on the sugar converting it into ethyl alcohol with the evolution of carbon dioxide. Other chemical substances are also formed in the process but they need not concern us, apart perhaps, from the production of small quantities of glycerol which augments the final smoothness of the wine.

Without yeast, no fermentation can take place and no alcohol can be produced. Old fashioned 'no yeast' recipes depended on the action of wild yeasts present on the ingredients and in the air. These yeasts are unreliable and unsatisfactory for winemaking purposes since most of them do not have the alcohol tolerance to ferment a wine to dryness, and they may impart an undesirable off-flavour and bouquet.

Bakers and brewers yeasts were widely used by country winemakers 15–20 years ago, but as our craft has gained popularity and expertise, so the manufacturers of winemaking products have sought to provide us with a wide selection of true wine yeasts. These are much superior to brewers and bakers yeasts which can impart bread-like and beery flavours to wine and generally have a poorer alcohol tolerance.

Although wine yeasts are very closely related to bakers and brewers yeasts, their behaviour does differ considerably. The yeast of choice for winemaking is *Saccharomyces Cerevisiae* var. *Ellipsoides*. There are many different strains of this yeast, each one being characteristic of the variety of grape from which it was obtained and the conditions in the wine producing region in which the grape is grown.

Much scientific work has been done on the selection and growth of cultures of these different yeasts which are now readily available in dried or liquid form, or as cultures on agar slopes. The form most commonly used is the dried granular types although the other two types are thought to be purer and therefore give better results. If one wishes to produce a Chablis type wine, a Chablis yeast may be used; for a Sauternes type wine, a Sauternes yeast or Chateau d'Yquem yeast may be used; a sherry type wine, for preference, requires a sherry yeast and so on. These specific yeasts should help to impart the characteristic flavour and bouquet of the wine type, providing that suitable flavour ingredients have been chosen in the first instance.

Generally speaking, until a winemaker becomes reasonably experienced, *all-purpose* yeasts are the best type to use. These are a blend of many strains and are usually very good. Many experienced winemakers (myself included) regularly use all-purpose yeasts believing that they gain little in wine quality by utilising the specialised yeasts. It would be of considerable interest to make two separate batches of wine from the same ingredients and ferment one with an all-purpose yeast and the other with the yeast best suited to the type of wine one is attempting to make. On maturity of the wine, samples could be compared and any differences in flavour and bouquet noted.

There are a few all-purpose yeasts (available in packets, tubs or jars) which can be prepared for introduction into the must in only six hours. These yeasts are normally dried, granular types and are mixed with a little nutrient in the pack. One or two teaspoonsful of such yeasts are mixed with a few fluid ounces of water in a sterilised bottle plugged with cotton wool or covered by a tissue. The 'starter bottle' as it is called, is put in a warm place (70°F. or 21°C.) for six hours, by which time sound fermentation will be observed. The starter is then ready to be introduced into the must.

It is always beneficial to prepare a starter bottle to encourage good yeast growth before adding the yeast to the must. If yeast is added directly to the must in its dry state, fermentation may take quite a few *days* to commence, as opposed to *12–24 hours* when a starter is used. The sooner fermentation begins the more encouraging it is, for beginners particularly. Some of the specific yeasts take a few days to establish fermentation in the must.

All-purpose yeasts normally have a high alcohol tolerance so that strong wines, containing 16–18% alcohol, may be obtained if desired.

When fermentation ceases these yeasts tend to settle out well to a firm deposit, called the lees. This facilitates racking procedures and clarification of the wine is usually fairly rapid.

Preparing a Starter Bottle (for other than the yeasts mentioned above)

When specific yeasts are used, they usually have to be made up into a nutritious starter a *few days* before introduction into the must, so that a strong yeast colony is established.

A suitable starter medium may be prepared as follows:

1 dessertspoonful of sugar.

¼ teaspoonful of citric acid (or acid mixture).

A pinch of yeast nutrient.

¼ pint (142 ml.) of water.

Dissolve the sugar in the water by warming. When the liquor is cool add to the acid, nutrient, and the yeast of choice, in a sterilised bottle and plug the bottle with cotton wool or cover with a tissue. Place in a warm position (70°F. or 21°C.) for a few days until fermentation is strongly under way. (i.e. frothing is observed). It may then be added to the must.

A very economical method, that can be used with any yeasts, is to feed the starter bottle every few days with a fresh starter medium. This is very useful if the winemaker is making wine regularly, say once a week:

Instead of introducing the *whole* of the starter to a must, keep a little back and add freshly prepared starter medium Yeast growth will continue and a vigorous colony will be built up within a few days. Most of this may be used for the next batch of wine and the remainder may be replenished as before. Thus, one lot of yeast may be kept in an active state, ready for use every few days. A starter may be kept going for quite a few weeks in this way.

Alternatively, after adding most of a yeast starter to a wine, the remainder may be put in the refrigerator where activity will die down and the yeast will become dormant. When required, it should be replenished with starter medium and put in a warm place for a few days, by which time a strong yeast colony should be seen to have developed—it is then ready for use again.

The lees (sediment) from a finished batch of wine can be utilised to make a starter for new musts. It is preferable to use the lees from the *second* racking rather than the first, since the latter usually contains decaying fruit pulp and much dead yeast. It is *not* advisable to use lees in this way unless no fresh yeast is available, because the yeast is in a considerably weakened state after fermentation. Off-flavours may result, particularly if lees from the first racking are used.

There are some very useful and interesting yeasts available for use in special circumstances. One firm has produced a *cold* fermentation yeast capable of withstanding temperatures as low as 40°F. (4°C.). This is a handy yeast for winter winemaking if one does not have a warm fermentation cupboard, or thermostatically controlled heaters in the wine and there is nowhere constantly warm enough for good fermentation in the home. Usually, however, one can get by using normal yeasts although fermentation may take considerably longer than usual in cold weather. The optimum temperature for fermentation, using ordinary yeasts is 60°F.–70°F. (16°C.–21°C.).

Another yeast of interest is one which reduces the malic acid content of a wine during fermentation. This can be very useful when making wine from gooseberries, sour apples, unripe plums, damsons, grapes or greengages which are normally very acid fruits containing mainly malic acid. The final acidity of the wine is much more acceptable to the palate when this yeast is utilised and it replaces the need for adding chalk or potassium carbonate to reduce the normally high acidity of such wines.

Many books advise the use of malt extract in starter mediums, but because of a major disaster in my own experience, I stopped this practice. Malt extract *is* very nutritious and does help to promote good yeast growth but there is a great danger, as my story will reveal. Years ago, I was in the habit of feeding my yeast starter, keeping it going for many weeks as described above, but in addition to the starter ingredients mentioned, I used a little malt extract also. One day, I ran out of malt extract, purchased a new jar and continued feeding my starter bottle until, at the stage of preparing the medium for my thirteenth consecutive gallon of wine, I noticed that the malt extract had a strange smell! To my horror, on examining the label on the jar, I discovered that the contents included *cod-liver oil*! I allowed the 13 gallons to mature, hoping that the cod-liver oil would float to the surface or sink to the bottom of each jar. No such luck! Each wine tasted absolutely revolting and had to be poured down the sink. So, be warned! If you wish to use malt extract in a starter medium, read the label first to make sure that it does not contain cod-liver oil.

One dessertspoonful of malt extract dissolved with the sugar in water, is the requirement for a really nutritious starter medium. Add all other ingredients as described before.

Fermentation, when established in a must, will not continue indefinitely. It will cease when either:

(a) there is no more sugar for the yeast to feed on (i.e. all the sugar has been converted into alcohol).

or (b) the alcohol tolerance of the yeast has been reached and it subsequently dies. The alcohol tolerance of different yeasts does vary quite considerably. All purpose yeasts, with careful feeding, can normally produce 17-18% alcohol by volume, whereas the specific yeasts meant for table wine production, may only tolerate about 11-13%.

The process of fermentation is discussed in some detail in the next chapter.

(10) YEAST NUTRIENTS

Yeast is a living organism which requires nutrients and

vitamins to enable it to work correctly to produce sound fermentation and wine of good quality.

As far as nutrients are concerned, its requirements are mainly *ammonium phosphate* and *ammonium sulphate* which are to be found in most proprietary brands of yeast nutrient. These substances provide the necessary nitrogen and phosphates required to promote good yeast growth and sound fermentation.

One level teaspoonful of yeast nutrient is required per gallon (4.5 litres) of wine.

The ammonium phosphate and ammonium sulphate may be purchased separately, in bulk, from chemists or good winemaking suppliers. It is much more economical to do this than to buy the proprietary brands of yeast nutrient. If these substances are acquired in this way, the following proportions of each should be used:

$\frac{1}{2}$ teaspoonful of ammonium phosphate per gallon (4.5 litres) of wine, plus: $\frac{1}{2}$ teaspoonful of ammonium sulphate per gallon (4.5 litres) of wine.

Some winemakers like to use *potassium phosphate* to ensure that the yeast has an adequate supply of necessary potassium salts. These are often present naturally in musts but occasionally there may be a deficiency. If one wishes to use potassium phosphate:

$\frac{1}{4}$–$\frac{1}{2}$ teaspoonful is adequate for 1 gallon (4.5 litres) of wine.

In soft-water areas the addition of a pinch of *magnesium sulphate* (Epsom salts) will aid fermentation, but it is not essential.

Vitamins

Vitamin B_1 or B compound is extremely helpful (although not absolutely essential) in ensuring a sound fermentation when used in addition to the nutrients mentioned above. These tablets may be obtained from any chemists and are extremely cheap. One warning—do not let the sales girl supply you with a bottle of *Brewers yeast* tablets which do contain the B vitamins, but also the undesirable brewers yeast.

One 3 mg. tablet suffices for 1 gallon (4.5 litres) of fruit or vegetable wine.

When making flower wines which have little natural nutrition in them, it is wise to use 2×3 mg. vitamin B_1 or B compound tablets to assist the yeast activity.

If 3 mg. size tablets are not available, larger ones may be used.

Yeast Energiser

This is a concentrated yeast food, often containing 20 to 30 trace elements, salts and vitamins which yeast requires for growth and sound fermentation. Most of the ingredients in yeast energiser are provided naturally by the contents of fruit and vegetable musts, but flower wines may be deficient. It is very advantageous to add yeast energiser, together with nutrients and vitamin B to flower wines. This should ensure that fermentation progresses well.

Directions on the container should be followed as to the amounts to use. Usually only $\frac{1}{4}$ teaspoonful is necessary.

Yeast energiser is often very useful in the case of a stuck fermentation. The addition of a little energiser will often boost the dormant yeast into activity once more.

Yeast nutrients (and vitamin B) should be added to *every* gallon (4.5 litres) of wine since deficient musts will cause the yeast to produce undesirable by-products, such as the fusel-oils, which create off-flavours in the wine.

(11) PECTIN DESTROYING ENZYME

Pectin is present in considerable but varying amounts in all fruits, while vegetables also contain a certain amount. It is pectin which makes jam set, so one can imagine that if fruits or vegetables are boiled (when preparing the must), the pectin content of the juice will be high. In the extreme, a juice having a very high pectin content may be jelly-like in consistency—obviously undesirable in wine. Banana 'gravy', when produced by boiling or pressure-cooking over-ripe bananas, often becomes jelly-like on cooling.

Even if the ingredients are not boiled, pouring boiling water over them will cause some pectin to be released into the must.

The presence of pectin in a wine will invariably prevent that wine from becoming crystal clear after fermentation. A slight, opaque haze will be apparent, even though all yeast may have settled out.

Prevention is better than cure, therefore it is wise to use a pectin-destroying enzyme in the preparation of every wine utilising fruit or vegetable of any kind.

These enzymes are available in liquid and powder forms. There are various different brands and the concentration of the products differs. Each has its own instructions as to the amount to use and these should be carefully followed.

Since enzymes are destroyed by heat, they should not be added to a must until the liquid is at *room temperature*. They should be put into the must at the same time as the Campden tablet or sulphite solution (when using Method 1 or 2, described in Chapter VI), 24 hours before adding the yeast. They aid in the breakdown of the fruit and consequently increase juice extraction during pulp fermentation.

Pectin destroying enzymes can be added to a finished wine which is found to have a pectin haze. It will remove the haze and will not adversely affect the flavour or quality of the wine. A precipitate is formed and this should be allowed to settle before the wine is racked into a fresh jar.

(12) WATER

As far as making wine is concerned, the softness or hardness of the water seems to have little effect on fermentation or wine quality. Hard water may have the advantage of containing traces of magnesium sulphate (Epsom salts) which is required in small amounts by the yeast. It is said that fermentation proceeds more slowly when a wine is produced from soft water, but this can be rectified quite easily by adding a pinch of magnesium sulphate (Epsom salts) as mentioned previously.

Cold tap water is generally thought to be pure enough for all winemaking needs. Boiling is not necessary and in fact, not desirable when preparing a must, since the dissolved oxygen is removed during the process, and fermentation requires as much oxygen as possible during the first few days.

Now that all the facts and figures have been discussed in detail, the winemaker is ready to formulate his or her own recipes or adjust (if necessary) ones obtained from other sources.

Preparation of the must and its future management will be described in the next chapter.

CHAPTER VI

THE 'must' is the combination of ingredients from which the wine is made. Its preparation is the most critical stage in wine-making, since the final quality of the wine will depend on the correct balance of ingredients (as discussed in previous chapters) incorporated in the initial preparation of the must. It should therefore be decided beforehand what type of wine is desired, and a sensible choice of ingredients be made in order to achieve the appropriate characteristics.

All equipment should be cleaned thoroughly, and rinsed with stock sulphite solution followed by cold tap water. All fruit or vegetables preferably should be fully ripe and in good condition so that they have attained full flavour and maturity. If any bruised, decaying or mouldy patches are discovered on inspection, meticulous removal is necessary in order to prevent off-flavours and contamination of the must by bacteria. Thorough washing of the ingredients should follow, to remove dust, dirt and possibly harmful residues from fungicidal or insecticidal sprays. However it must be said that the washing of very juicy fruits such as elderberries is not really practicable, as much of their juice would be lost in the process.

As a general rule, very over-ripe, poor quality fruit should be avoided because of the possibility of introducing infections into the wine, but if they are used in the must, it should be fairly heavily sulphited (two Campden tablets or 10 ml. stock sulphite solution) prior to adding the yeast. 'Black' or spotted, over-ripe bananas provide one of the few exceptions to this rule, since they attain their best flavour and sugar content in this condition, and their undesirable starch content is much reduced.

Flowers should be picked on a dry, sunny day, and should be fully open so that their perfume is at its best. All stalks and greenery are best removed or a bitter flavour may be obtained. It is preferable *not* to wash flowers, otherwise a fair amount of their fragrance may be lost. The only exception to this might be garden rose petals on which insecticide sprays are known to have been used. Incidentally, on gathering a bucket full of flowers, it will be found that quite a collection of insect life has also been obtained, but do not let this be off-putting. There is no easy way to remove these bugs and beasties, but their presence initially does not appear to affect the quality of the finished wine in my experience.

All the ingredients being to hand, it must be decided which method to follow to extract the flavour from the fruit, vegetables or flowers. There are three basic methods used by the majority of winemakers, of which the first is the most popular. All three follow the basic 'seven pints (4 litres) method' as described in Chapter V, so that the S.G. table can be used to calculate future sugar additions.

METHOD 1. INFUSION METHOD

This procedure is mainly intended for soft (or semi-soft) vegetables, fruits, flowers, grain and tinned or bottled fruits. Citrus fruits are not normally dealt with by this method, and more will be said about these later.

Fruits should be chopped up into small pieces, crushed, coarsely minced or lightly liquidised, so that the maximum flavour may be obtained. Any large pips or stones should be removed, as these would tend to give a bitter flavour to the wine, but generally it is unnecessary to core apples and pears as long as care is taken not to cut the pips. Grape pips may safely be ignored, as may cherry stones—mainly because of the tedious business of removing the latter.

The prepared fruit or flowers are put into a sterilised bucket and a *measured* amount, say 2–3 pints (1 or 1½ litres) of boiling water is poured over the mass. The bucket should be covered with a cloth, a sheet of fine polythene held on with an elastic band, or a fairly well fitting (but not completely airtight) lid, and left until the liquor is cool. A crushed Campden tablet or one 5 ml. teaspoon of stock sulphite solution and the pectin destroying enzyme are then added, and the vessel re-covered and left 24 hours for the sulphite to destroy wild yeasts and bacteria. After 24 hours the rest of the recipe ingredients are added, and since the effect of the sulphite will have diminished considerably, the prepared yeast starter may be put in without its activity being impaired. A careful check should be kept on the volume of liquids added to the must, and the total liquid content made up to 7 pints (4 litres) with cold tap water (see Chapter V, pp. 55). This 7 pint (4 litre) measure therefore will contain some or all of the following:

(a) the estimated or measured quantity of natural juice in the fruit;
(b) the amount of boiling water used;
(c) the volume of sugar syrup;
(d) the tannin, if added as cold tea;
(e) the yeast starter;
(f) cold tap water to bring the total to 7 pints (4 litres).

Estimating the volume of juice one expects to obtain from fruits is difficult and really only comes with experience. Much depends on the condition of the particular fruit, but the following will give a rough idea for the most commonly used ingredients. (Flowers, of course, have a negligible liquid content.)

4 lb. apples or pears	approx. 1–1¼ pints
(1.81 kilos)	(0.57–0.71 litres)
3 lb. elderberries	approx. 1½ pints
(1.36 kilos)	(0.85 litres)
3 lb. blackberries	approx. 1¼ pints
(1.36 kilos)	(0.71 litres)
3 lb. sloes	approx. ¾ pint
(1.36 kilos)	(0.43 litres)
5 lb. grapes	approx. 2 pints
(2.27 kilos)	(1.14 litres)
5 lb. marrow	approx. 2½ pints
(2.27 kilos)	(1.42 litres)
4 lb. plums or peaches	approx. 1½ pints
(1.81 kilos)	(0.85 litres)
3 lb. rosehips	approx. 1 pint
(1.36 kilos)	(0.57 litres).

It is worth noting here that it is of no benefit to mark the bucket at the 7 pint (4 litre) level because the volume of fruit pulp will increase the total volume occupied by the must to well over such a mark.

Include only 2–2½ lb. (0.91–1.13 kilos) of *total* sugar in

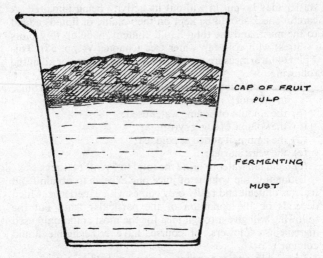

CAP OF FRUIT
PULP

FERMENTING
MUST

Fig. 8   Cross-section of Bucket with Fermenting Must

making up the initial must (see Chapter V, p. 60) since more
than the latter quantity present at this stage may cause a
stuck fermentation later.

Once all the desired ingredients are in the bucket, stir very
thoroughly with a long handled wood or plastic spoon. Next
take out a sample of the liquor, strain it through a nylon sieve
to remove pulp debris, take a hydrometer reading and note it
down. Subtract this reading from the appropriate figure for
the wine type in Table 1 (column 4) on page 59. The number of
points of difference between these two figures is the number of
tablespoonsful of strong sugar syrup (SSS) to be added in
stages during the fermentation once the original sugar has been
converted into alcohol.

Return the sample of must to the bucket, cover, put in a
warm place at approximately 70°F. (21°C.) and stir twice daily
for three to five days. During these first few days, fermentation
(which normally starts within 12–24 hours) is very vigorous
and the sheer force of the carbon dioxide gas evolved drives
the pulp to the surface of the must to form a compact 'cap'.

It is very important that this cap be broken up and mixed thoroughly with the rest of the must, partly to facilitate flavour and colour extraction from the pulp, and partly to keep it moist and free from bacterial infection.

After three to five days, whenever it is convenient, strain the fermenting liquor through a nylon sieve, nylon straining bag, or muslin, into a clean gallon jar: check and note the S.G., check the acidity and adjust if necessary, and fit a bored cork and air-lock containing $\frac{1}{2}-\frac{3}{4}$ in. ($1\frac{1}{2}$–2 cm.) depth of sulphite solution. Label the jar and place it in a slightly cooler position than previously, at approximately 60°F. (15.5°C.). Agitating the jar once daily, if possible, leave it to continue this quieter, secondary fermentation which may take a few weeks or even months, making sugar additions when necessary (Chapter V, pp. 62–64). Details of future management may be found in later pages.

For the sake of clarity, the following is a brief summary of the important stages of Method 1.

(a) Prepare fruit, vegetable or flowers and put in bucket.

(b) Pour over measured amount of boiling water; cool.

(c) Add one crushed Campden tablet or 5 ml. stock sulphite solution and pectin-destroying enzyme; cover, and leave for 24 hours.

(d) Add all other recipe ingredients: take S.G. reading, and calculate sugar additions.

(e) Ferment at 70°F. (21°C.) stirring regularly, for three to five days.

(f) Strain into gallon jar, and fit cork and air-lock. Check acidity and adjust if necessary.

(g) Ferment on at 60°F. (15.5°C.), agitating once daily.

METHOD 2. COLD WATER METHOD

This method of extracting flavour may be used for the same types of ingredients as in Method 1, but apart from a few exceptions has less to recommend it. Using cold water is unlikely to extract as much flavour or colour from the fruit or flowers. However, there are some authorities who insist that this method is best, since they believe that using the infusion method imparts a 'cooked' flavour to the wine. My own experience does not support this contention.

The ingredients for which this method is almost essential, are those which oxidise and turn brown very rapidly in contact with air—for example large quantities of apples and pears (although Method 1 can be used happily for the relatively small amounts of fruit needed for only a single gallon (4.5 litres) of wine).

Two or three pints of cold water should be put into a sterile bucket, and a crushed Campden tablet (dissolved by warming in a little of the water) or 5 ml. of stock sulphite solution and the pectin-destroying enzyme added. The fruit is then put into the sulphited water as each piece is prepared, browning being prevented by the short period of exposure to the air, and the action of the sulphite.

The bucket should be covered and left for 24 hours, the remainder of the recipe ingredients then added, and the whole made up to total liquid content of 7 pints (4 litres). The S.G. reading is taken, and the process continued as in Method 1. The summary is as follows:

(a) Place 2–3 pints cold water in the bucket.
(b) Add crushed Campden tablet or 5 ml. stock sulphite solution and pectin-destroying enzyme;
(c) Prepare and add fruit to sulphited water. Cover and leave 24 hours.
(d) Add all other recipe ingredients, make up to 7 pints (4 litres) total liquid. Take S.G. reading and calculate sugar additions.
(e) Proceed as from Method 1, (e).

METHOD 3. BOILING METHOD

This is used mainly for very hard fruits, root vegetables, most dried fruits that require to be reconstituted, and bananas (included here in view of the excessive structural breakdown of the fruit that would occur during pulp fermentation).

Because of the likelihood of imparting a 'cooked' flavour to the wine, this method should be avoided for all but the types of ingredients mentioned above. Also, cooking will release large amounts of pectin into the juice, leading to possible difficulties in clearing the wine, so that the use of a pectin-destroying enzyme becomes essential.

Chop up the fruit or vegetables. Dried fruit should be

minced or lightly liquidised. Place it in a nylon straining bag tied around the top, and put into a large pan with about 3 pints (1½ litres) of water. Bring to the boil, and simmer for the normal cooking time (approximately 20 minutes for fruit and vegetables, or 45 minutes to 1 hour for dried fruits.)

It is a debatable point whether or not the pan should be covered during cooking. Some authorities think that it is better to leave the pan open so that some undesirable volatile substances may be drive off in the steam, while others hold that a lot of flavour will be lost unless the too free escape of steam is prevented by the use of a lid. I incline towards the latter view.

A pressure cooker may be used if so desired, in which case the prepared ingredient in the tied straining bag is placed in the cooker with no more than 2 pints of water. The cooker is brought up to 15 lb./in.^{2} pressure, and held there for the normal cooking time (five minutes for fruit and vegetables, or 15–20 minutes for dried fruits).

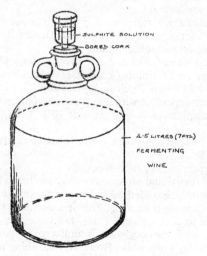

Fig. 9   Demijohon with Airlock

In either method, bananas are cooked for the same length of time as fresh fruit or vegetables.

After cooking for the required length of time, remove the straining bag and hang it up to drain. Measure the volume of the liquid, since it will have diminished somewhat during cooking (especially if an open pan has been used).

When cool, pour the liquid into a sterile gallon jar. No sulphiting will be necessary in this case, as the cooking will have effectively killed off any bacteria.

Add all the other recipe ingredients as in Method 1, making the total liquid volume up to 7 pints (4 litres), check acidity and adjust if necessary, and take the S.G. reading. Cover the neck of the jar with a tissue or elastic band, or plug it with cotton wool, and put in a warm place at approximately 70°F. (21°C.), agitating once or twice daily, for three to five days. Replace the tissue or cotton wool with a bored cork and air-lock, and move the jar to a slightly cooler place, ideally about 60°F. (15.5°C.) for the remainder of the fermentation period, as in Method 1. The summary is as follows:

(a) Prepare fruit or veg.

(b) Place in a tied straining bag, in pan or pressure cooker.

(c) Cook for normal cooking or reconstituting time.

(d) Drain off and collect liquor.

(e) Pour into gallon jar and add all other recipe ingredients. Make up to 7 pints (4 litres), take S.G. and calculate sugar addition. Check acidity and adjust if necessary.

(f) Cover neck of jar with tissue, or insert cotton wool plug.

(g) Ferment three to five days at 70°F. (21°C.). Agitate daily.

(h) Fit cork and air-lock. Move to temperature of 60°F. (15.5°C.).

(i) Ferment on, agitating once daily.

It is up to individual winemakers which method is employed, but the majority find Method 1 of most constant use.

Electric juice extractors or fruit presses may be used to extract the juice from some fruits, but these are, of course, expensive, and the beginner is unlikely to consider the financial outlay worthwhile. However, flourishing wine circles may have such equipment available on loan to members for a small fee.

If juice is extracted by one of these means, it should be sulphited immediately in the receiving vessel to prevent oxidation and contamination. The volume of juice obtained should then be measured, the acidity checked and adjusted if necessary, and the must prepared and dealt with as in Method 3, since there would be no pulp fermentation.

SPECIAL CASES

Some ingredients require special attention—particularly citrus fruits and rhubarb. In the former case, the white pith should never be included, as it imparts an extremely bitter taste to the must. The outer peel should be finely grated, boiled for five minutes in a pint ($\frac{1}{2}$ litre) of water, and left for 24 hours to extract maximum flavour. The (halved) fruit is squeezed, the juice collected, and its volume measured. It is then poured into a sterile gallon jar, and a Campden tablet or 5 ml. of stock sulphite solution added. The neck of the jar is covered with a tissue or plugged with cotton wool, and it is left to stand for 24 hours. Next day the liquor is strained from the peel, and added to the juice in the jar together with all the other recipe ingredients. From here on, the procedure follows Method 3.

Rhubarb needs special attention because of its toxic oxalic acid content. Some winemakers actually advise ignoring the presence of oxalic acid, believing that the amount extracted by cold water is too slight to be harmful, and proceed to prepare the must as in Method 2. Others, myself included, prefer to remove the oxalic acid by precipitation with chalk before adding the usual citric acid or acid mixture. This is best done by chopping up the rhubarb, putting it into a sterile bucket with 2 or 3 pints (1–1$\frac{1}{2}$ litres) of cold water, a Campden tablet or 5 ml. sulphite solution, and 1 oz. (28 gm.) of precipitated chalk. The bucket is covered, and stirred daily for two to three days before the liquor is strained off into a clean gallon jar. After allowing to stand for a few hours, the juice is racked off the sediment into another jar, and the rest of the ingredients added, including the full amount of acid.

FERMENTATION PROCESS

Fermentation is the process whereby yeast converts the

sugar in the must to alcohol and carbon dioxide, together with small quantities of a few by-products.

A sound fermentation is dependent upon the correct preparation of the must. The action of yeast in *any* sugary juice will produce an alcoholic drink, but unless controlled quantities of such ingredients as sugar and acid are used, the end product may be far from pleasant, due to adverse effects on the fermentation process. A little commonsense and care, however, will almost always ensure good results.

The process may be divided into two distinct phases.

(1) Primary Fermentation

This stage should be conducted in AEROBIC conditions (i.e. in the presence of air) since it is a time of very rapid yeast growth—and yeast, being a living organism, requires oxygen from the air in order to obtain the energy necessary for growth. To assist aeration of the must, the bucket used for the first few days is covered with a cloth, polythene, or a loosely fitting lid (or in the case of a gallon jar, the neck is covered with tissue or plugged with cotton wool). The establishment of a good yeast colony is essential if the fermentation is to proceed to completion.

A temperature of approximately 70°F. (21°C.) is ideal for these first few days, although a few degrees either way will not affect the yeast activity to a great extent. However the temperature should never exceed 80°F. (26.7°C.) or the yeast cells will be killed and fermentation will cease.

Finding suitable places to put fermenting wines is occasionally a problem, but a south-facing room is useful since even during the winter it will be warm on sunny days. Many people use the airing cupboard, but a warning note must be sounded here. If the door is shut, the temperature can become far too high, with the danger of killing the yeast, or, if not that, at least causing too rapid fermentation. Leaving the door slightly ajar, permitting the circulation of air, may create the desired conditions.

Primary fermentations last three to ten days, the average being five. It may be a few hours or even a day or two before the start of the fermentation becomes obvious, but when really established the force of the carbon dioxide gas being given off pushes the fruit pulp up in the bucket (when using

Methods 1 and 2) to form a cap on top of the liquid. This cap should be broken up and stirred into the must twice daily if possible, for reasons explained in previous pages. If the fermentation is beginning in a gallon jar, frothing will be seen to occur in most cases, especially on agitation of the liquid.

Alcohol production is considerable at this stage, and it is quite common, if conditions are favourable, for the S.G. of the must to drop from say 1.080 to 1.015 in about five days, indicating that almost 2 lb. (0.91 kilo) of sugar has been converted into alcohol by the yeast. However, the rate of gravity drop is variable and dependent upon many factors.

When a strong fermentation is established, usually in three to five days, the carbon dioxide that has been produced will occupy the space in the vessel above the must, cutting off the air supply, so that yeast activity slows and the fermentation gradually subsides to a steadier rate. It is at this point that the pulp is strained off if the must has been prepared as in Methods 1 or 2, and the liquor is transferred to a sterile gallon jar. This stage marks the beginning of the secondary fermentation.

Before leaving this section, however, it should be mentioned that all wines should be kept out of direct sunlight, as this adversely affects the fermentation. Red wines, in addition, should be kept completely covered or put in a dark place—otherwise the colour has a tendency to fade to tawny brown.

(2) Secondary Fermentation

This stage, which lasts a few weeks or even months, is conducted under ANAEROBIC conditions, due to the blanket of carbon dioxide gas above the must. Since it is also necessary to prevent flies and bacteria gaining access to the liquor in the gallon jar, it is wise to fit a bored cork and airlock containing some sulphite solution.

The ideal temperature at which to conduct this phase is approximately 60°F. (15.5°C.). Higher temperatures, in the range 70°F. (21°C.)–80°F. (26.7°C.) increase the rate of fermentation too much, with consequent deterioration in the quality of the wine. Temperatures of 55°F. (12.8°C.) and below may slow the fermentation to such an extent that the yeast may very well go into hibernation, and fermentation may cease altogether. Wide fluctuations in temperature should be avoided if possible, but without financial outlay on thermostatic methods of control, this becomes very difficult.

The secondary fermentation is much slower than the primary but a steady rising of bubbles is evident on close inspection, accompanied by an intermittent 'blooping' of the air-lock. Agitation of the jar once daily keeps the yeast working throughout the must, and prevents it from being buried by pulp debris.

An S.G. reading should be taken at the end of the primary fermentation, and then every five to seven days during the secondary, to record the progress of the conversion of sugar into alcohol. It will be found that the S.G. drops very rapidly during the first few days, gradually slowing as the amount of sugar available for the yeast to feed on decreases. It is when a S.G. reading of 1.000 or below is obtained that feeding of the yeast, in stages, by the addition of sugar syrup, is commenced. Up to five to 10 tablespoonsful may be added at a time, usually at weekly intervals under ideal temperature conditions, as long as the must continues to ferment and the S.G. drops to 1.000 or below between successive additions. As time passes, the fermentation may slow down to such an extent that it may be necessary to wait more than a week between the last few sugar additions.

Following the addition of all the extra sugar syrup to be used (see Chapter V, p.61) the fermentation should be stopped when the S.G. drops to the required level (for example, to 1.000 or below for a really dry wine, or to between 1.000 and 1.010 for a medium wine). A sweet table, social, or dessert wine probably will require a little extra sugar syrup to bring the S.G. up to between 1.010 and 1.020 before fermentation is brought to a halt.

In the case of social or dessert wines, the limit of the alcohol tolerance of the yeast may be reached before *all* the extra sugar can be added, and the fermentation will consequently cease. Any further sugar additions, therefore, would only serve to sweeten the wine further, possible beyond the desired level. If this should happen, then the alcohol level has to be accepted as the preferred alternative, though fortification with spirit can be undertaken if so wished.

Assuming that the wine has now reached the point at which it is desired to stop the fermentation, or when it ceases of its own accord, it should be left for a day to settle, and then be racked, as described below, to remove most of the yeast.

RACKING AND MATURING

It is vital that the wine be racked off the lees as soon as fermentation has either reached completion, or when it has reached the desired finishing point. The most important reason for this is that the dead yeast cells and pulp debris begin to decompose by way of a process called autolysis with consequent production of off flavours and undesirable fusel oils.

The jar of wine to be racked should carefully be placed on a table or bench so as not to disturb the sediment, and a sterile, empty jar is placed below so that the bottom of the upper jar is at a higher level than the top of the lower jar (see diagram Fig. 10 p. 97).

The simplest method of racking is to use 1.5 yards (1.5 metres) of polythene or rubber siphon tubing of $\frac{1}{4}$ in. (6 mm.) diameter. One end of the tubing is carefully dipped into the wine so as not to disturb the sediment or lees. Wine is now sucked up to fill the tube, and, with a finger held firmly over the free end, the tube is bent over and lowered towards the second jar. Releasing the finger when the free end is below the base of the first jar, the tube is lowered to near the base of the second jar, allowing the liquid to siphon down into the latter. A free flow of wine from the upper jar to the lower will continue as long as the upper end of the tube remains below the surface of the liquor in the upper jar. When there is only a little wine left in the latter, it should be gently tipped at an angle so that as much of the liquid and as little sediment as possible is removed.

Top up the lower jar to just below the cork with cold water, add a crushed Campden tablet or 5 ml. of stock strong sulphite solution and replace the cork and air-lock. This removal of the bulk of the yeast and sulphiting of the wine severely inhibits the fermentation, which will cease within a few days.

Some authorities are so fastidious about the employment of sterile techniques that they insist on using only cool boiled

97

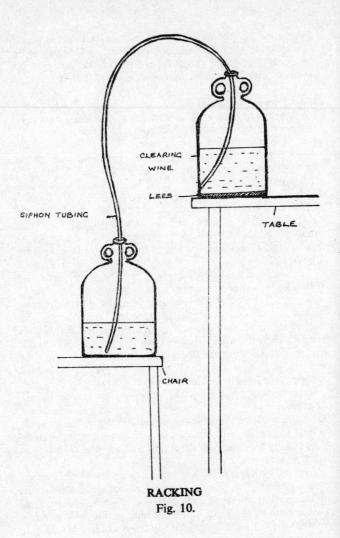

RACKING
Fig. 10.

water for topping up jars. Personally I have never gone to such lengths, and I have not had the misfortune to see any serious bacterial infections develop in my wines. Cold tap water is generally considered to be sufficiently pure by most winemakers.

The jar should now be stored in a cool dark place at approximately 50°F. (10°C.) for the maturing stage. The garage, the cupboard under the stairs, a north-facing room, or even under the floorboards provide suitable places. During this time the yeast gradually settles out to the bottom of the jar, and the wine becomes progressively clearer from the top downwards. Remember particularly to keep red wines in the dark or covered to prevent loss of colour.

Rack for the second time about four weeks after the first, or sooner if another heavy deposit is thrown down. The jar is again topped up with cold water, a crushed Campden tablet or 5 ml. of strong sulphite solution added, and the cork and air-lock replaced. Take care to check regularly that the air-lock still contains sufficient sulphite solution to prevent spoilage organisms gaining entry to the wine. It may even be advisable occasionally to replace the sulphite solution, which may gradually lose its effectiveness, due to atmospheric oxidation. On a cautionary note, beware the insidiously intoxicating effect of 'shiphoning sheveral gallons of wine at a shingle sheshion!'

The jar should now be put away again in a cool place. It will be noted that the wine, if not clear at this time, will be considerably less cloudy than fomerly. Subsequent rackings are indicated when any further yeast deposit appears, probably at two or three monthly intervals, until the wine is completely clear.

Sulphite is only added following the first two rackings, since a total of three Campden tablets or 15 ml. of sulphite solution is the maximum advisable concentration per gallon unless bacterial infection or re-fermentation occurs. Remember that in most wines one tablet or 5 ml. of stock sulphite solution is used in the preparation of the must.

Only when the wine is completely clear should the cork and air-lock be replaced by a plain cork. Corks are to be preferred to rubber bungs since the latter tend to perish due to the acidity of the wine, and stick to the neck of the jar. If fermentation should recommence, a rubber bung might not blow out, and the jar could explode, with possibly disastrous results. Cork is safer, but, just as important, it also allows small amounts of air to penetrate into the wine during the maturing phase. This is essential to facilitate the chemical changes that take place during maturation (which is better carried out in bulk, i.e. gallon or half-gallon (4.5 or 2.25 litre) jars, rather than in bottles for the first few months). It is often useful to transfer completely clear wines into half-gallon jars for initial maturation, leaving the demijohns free to accommodate new wines.

The clearing and racking of wines usually continues for two or three months, or possibly even longer. However as soon as the wine is crystal clear and free of all sediment, it may be consumed if desired. This stage normally is reached about four to six months after the initial preparation of the must. Beginners may find it hard to resist drinking the wine immediately it clears, but it is preferable to leave most wines to mature for at least a year, since the difference in quality between a six month and a one year old wine is quite considerable. Time smooths and mellows the wine, and enhances its bouquet.

A useful idea for beginners is to make a few more gallons of wine than they think that they will require, so that if half a gallon (2.25 litres) of each is drunk while still young, the other half may be put away for a few more months of maturation. It will be of considerable educational value to note down on the quality of the wine when still young, and compare them with those on the re-assessed wine after say a year's maturation.

In passing, I might mention that I have often been asked if repeated topping-up of the jar with water at each racking dilutes the wine too much. The answer to this is that in most cases it does not. This is because the amounts of ingredients in the recipes refer to 1 gallon of wine, and these are all originally contained in a total liquid volume of 7 pints (4 litres) which deliberately allows for the dilution effect that occurs during topping-up. In the case of dessert wines, however, which are required to be very high in alcohol content and very full-bodied, the winemaker is at liberty to top up the jar at rackings with a finished wine of the same type, to prevent dilution, should he so wish.

There are various gadgets other than the plain siphon tube on the market. Siphon pumps are available, but, of course, require a greater financial outlay, and are not really necessary. One easily obtainable refinement that some winemakers do like, is a glass U-tube fixed into the upper end of the siphon tube, which helps to prevent sucking up the lees.

BOTTLING

When the wine is completely clear and has matured in bulk for some months, it may be bottled.

It is wise to have a very critical tasting session beforehand, to assess any imbalances in the wine which may need correction by various means. Details of faults and imbalances frequently found, and how to correct or disguise them, are described in the next chapter, and these procedures should be carried out prior to bottling.

The wine should be completely stable—that is, it should show no tendency to re-ferment if put into a warm atmosphere for a few days; nor should a sample left standing in a glass for 24 hours darken in colour due to oxidation. These two simple tests are worth carrying out to make sure that the wine is ready. It is a wise precaution to add one sodium benzoate tablet, dissolved completely in a little of the wine, to each gallon a few days before bottling. This should prevent fermentation in the bottle.

Some winemakers like to add 200 mg. per gallon (4.5 litres) of Vitamin C (ascorbic acid) just prior to bottling, in addition to sodium benzoate. The latter substance inhibits fermentation, and the vitamin C prevents oxidation in the sealed bottles. Vitamin C tablets, 50 mg. size, are available at chemists, but unfortunately they do not dissolve very well, and leave a white deposit due to the binding agent in the tablets. It is preferable to buy pure ascorbic acid from a wine-making supplier. Ten gm. dissolved in 1 litre of water will give a stock solution from which 5×5 ml. teaspoonsful can be added to each gallon of wine prior to bottling.

Wine bottles have to be thoroughly cleaned and sterilised

before use. Silana p.f. is very useful for removing stains, but unfortunately tends to leave white streaky marks on the glass, which are unsightly. A solution of Domestos or Chempro S.D.P. in hot water is effective for all stains, and these are to be preferred as they do not mark the glass. Thorough rinsing with cold water should follow the use of any cleaning reagent, the bottles then being rinsed with a dilute sulphite solution, then water and allowed to drain for a while.

The wine is carefully racked into the bottles, leaving an air space of $\frac{1}{2}$–$\frac{3}{4}$ in. (13–19 mm.) below the cork. A strong clip on the siphon tube is useful to stop the flow of wine at the desired level.

Corks require softening before they can be driven into the neck of the bottles. This is best done by soaking them in a mild sulphite solution containing a little glycerine for two hours before they are needed. If required in a hurry, corks may be boiled in water containing a few drops of glycerine for a minute or so, to render them pliable. Boiling, however, does tend to make them rather brittle. For long-term storage, straight corks are the best choice, giving a very good seal. Flanged corks are useful only in the short term, as seepage of wine tends to occur during storage. Plastic topped corks cannot be boiled, since the plastic melts and becomes deformed.

A corking machine may be used to drive home straight corks, although it is quite simple to put them in by hand. A piece of string or a fine, bent skewer should be held in the neck of the bottle, and the cork pushed almost home with the handle of a wooden spoon. The skewer or string is then removed, and this allows a little air to escape before the cork is driven flush, thus preventing it from popping up again due to excess internal pressure.

Foil or viscose capsules are easily fitted over the necks of bottles, and do give them a professional finish. If foil capsules are used, a tool called a capsuler is necessary to secure a good fit.

The professional look can be completed by using one of the many attractive kinds of bottle label now available. Print on it the wine type (usually by ingredient), the date when made, and whether dry, medium or sweet.

Bottles should be stored on their sides so that the wine is in contact with the cork, keeping it moist and expanded—thus preventing the entry of bacteria. Wine racks can be bought, but again this incurs extra unnecessary expense. An old bookcase can be put to good use, or beer or milk crates may be stacked on their sides in a corner of the garage. The handyman, of course, will be able to erect some suitably strengthened shelves in the garage, where, if placed fairly high on the walls, they will not reduce garage space.

It must be remembered that the wine should be kept out of the light and as cool during bottle storage as during bulk storage, i.e. at approximately 50°F. (10°C.). Store the wine in bottles for a few months to complete maturation.

The shelf-life of home-made wines varies considerably. Some ingredients such as elderberries make a wine of particularly good keeping qualities. Flower wines, however, are usually so light and delicate that they are at their best at about nine months to a year, but after 18 months the beautiful bouquet that is the very essence of these wines will be found to have diminished somewhat. Basically, it all depends on how well balanced the wine is, since faults tend to become more pronounced at time goes by (hence the importance of attempting to formulate really sound recipes, and managing the fermentation and maturation stages with care). A good well balanced wine should maintain its quality for many years.

ASSESSING THE ALCOHOL CONTENT

Basically this is a very simple calculation provided that the following procedure is followed closely.

If the volume of a must *before* fermentation is 1 gallon (4.5 litres), it is only necessary to note the initial specific gravity (S.G.), and then the final S.G. after fermentation is complete. The final reading is subtracted from the initial S.G., omitting the decimal point, giving a figure which is the 'gravity drop'.

INITIAL S.G.−FINAL S.G.='GRAVITY DROP'

This 'gravity drop' is divided by 7.5 to give the approximate percentage of alcohol by volume.

Example

A must has an initial S.G. of 1.090, and the finished wine a S.G. of 1.000.

Now $1090 - 1000 = 90$.

90 is therefore the gravity drop, and $90/7.5 = 12$, so that the wine contains approximately 12% of alcohol.

However the 7 pint (4 litre) method of preparing the must, as described in this book, and the adding of sugar in stages during the fermentation complicates the calculation a little. The total amount of sugar in the finished gallon, and the corresponding S.G. that this would have given if all the sugar had been put in initially, must be worked out.

Table 3 can easily be used to calculate this inital S.G. in the following manner:

(1) Take the S.G. reading of the initial 7 pints (4 litres) of must, and multiply the *gravity* (i.e. the figures after the decimal point) by $\frac{7}{8}$ to obtain the S.G. that would have been recorded if the same amount of sugar had been in 1 gallon (4.5 litres).

(2) Read from the table the weight of sugar per gallon (4.5 litres) corresponding to this intial S.G.

(3) Multiply this weight by the number of gallons present in the initial must.

(4) Total up the number of tablespoonsful of sugar syrup added to the must in stages during the fermentation, and convert this figure into the corresponding actual *weight* of solid sugar. The following comparisons will be of help:

2 tablespoons S.S.S.* $= 1$ fluid oz. S.S.S.

40 tablespoons (20 fl. oz.) S.S.S. $= 1$ pint (0.57 litres) S.S.S.

40 tablespoons (20 fl. oz.) S.S.S. $= 1$ lb. (454 gm.) solid sugar.

Therefore 1 oz. (28 gm.) solid sugar $= 2\frac{1}{2}$ tablespoons S.S.S.

And the weight (in oz.) of sugar added $=$ No. of tablespoons S.S.S. $\times 2/5$.

*S.S.S. refers to the most concentrated solution of sugar that is possible—that is 1 lb. (454 gm.) sugar in $\frac{1}{2}$ pint (284 ml.) water, which gives 1 pint (568 ml.) strong sugar syrup (S.S.S.).

(5) Add this calculated weight of added sugar to the weight of sugar in the initial must, found in step 2).

(6) Divide this total weight of sugar by the number of gallons (4.5 litres) of *finished* wine.

(7) From the table, read the gravity corresponding to this

TABLE 3

Specific Gravity	Gravity	Weight of Sugar	
		(oz. per gallon)	(gm. per gallon)
1.000	0	$\frac{1}{2}$	(14)
1.005	5	$2\frac{3}{4}$	(78)
1.010	10	$4\frac{3}{4}$	(135)
1.015	15	7	(198)
1.020	20	9	(255)
1.025	25	11	(312)
1.030	30	$13\frac{1}{4}$	(376)
1.035	35	$15\frac{1}{2}$	(439)
1.040	40	$17\frac{1}{2}$	(496)
1.045	45	$19\frac{1}{2}$	(553)
1.050	50	$21\frac{1}{2}$	(610)
1.055	55	$23\frac{3}{4}$	(673)
1.060	60	$25\frac{3}{4}$	(730)
1.065	65	28	(794)
1.070	70	30	(850)
1.075	75	32	(907)
1.080	80	$34\frac{1}{4}$	(971)
1.085	85	$36\frac{1}{2}$	(1035)
1.090	90	$38\frac{1}{2}$	(1091)
1.095	95	$40\frac{1}{2}$	(1148)
1.100	100	$42\frac{3}{4}$	(1212)
1.105	105	45	(1276)
1.110	110	47	(1332)
1.115	115	49	(1389)
1.120	120	$51\frac{1}{4}$	(1452)
1.125	125	$53\frac{1}{4}$	(1508)
1.130	130	$55\frac{1}{2}$	(1571)
1.135	135	$57\frac{1}{2}$	(1627)
1.140	140	$59\frac{3}{4}$	(1690)
1.145	145	62	(1753)
1.150	150	64	(1809)
1.155	155	66	(1865)
1.160	160	$68\frac{1}{4}$	(1928)

weight of sugar. This would have been the gravity of the initial must, had all the sugar been put in at the start and the volume been made up to 1 gallon (4.5 litres) at that stage.

(8) Deduct the final gravity of the wine from the figure just obtained from the table. This gives the 'gravity drop'.

(9) Divide the 'gravity drop' by 7.5. This gives the approximate % alcohol by volume in the wine.

(10) To calculate° proof, multiply the % alcohol by 7/4.

At first sight, this may seem a very complicated calculation, but in fact this is not so. Step (4) is the only one which requires a little mathematics. The value for the % alcohol obtained in this way is not quite an accurate figure (due to factors too complicated to consider here) but it will serve as an adequate guide for the average winemaker.

The following is an example which will help to clarify matters.

1 gallon of a dry table wine was desired, so 7 pints (4 litres) of must were prepared, with an initial S.G. of 1.080.

(1) $80 \times 7/8 = 70$, therefore the initial S.G. of 1 gallon (4.5 litres) would have been 1.070.

(2) From the Table, 1.070 corresponds to 30 oz. (850 gm.) of sugar.

(3) Multiply by 1, since only 1 gallon (4.5 litres) is being prepared.

(4) 17 tablespoons of S.S.S. were added in all during the fermentation. Therefore weight of sugar added $= 17 \times 2/5 = 64/5$, or approximately $6\frac{3}{4}$ oz. (190 gm.).

(5) Initial sugar plus added sugar $= 30 + 6\frac{3}{4} = 36\frac{3}{4}$ oz. (1,040 gm.)

(6) Divide by 1, since only 1 gallon (4.5 litres) is being prepared.

(7) From Table, $36\frac{3}{4}$ oz. (1,040 gm.) corresponds to an initial S.G. of approximately 1.085.

(8) The finished S.G. of the wine was 1.002.
Therefore initial gravity − final gravity $= 85 - 2 = 83$.
This is the gravity drop.

(9) 83 divided by 7.5 gives about 11.1 % alcohol.

(10) $11.1 \times 7/4 = 77.7/4 = 19.4°$ proof.

CHAPTER VII

Faults and Diseases

Occasionally, no matter how careful and competent the winemaker, problems will arise with some wines. This chapter serves to pinpoint possible troubles and gives advice on how to resolve the situation. Although to a newcomer to winemaking, it may seem like a 'chamber of horrors!', there is no need for panic. Rarely does wine have to be thrown away.

FAULTS

(1) Stuck Fermentations

A fermentation is said to be 'stuck' when it has ceased prematurely at a point where the S.G. is too high for the wine to be drinkable. In other words, insufficient sugar has fermented out, leaving a syrupy, sickly sweet wine. A wine having a S.G. of anything above 1.025 is generally considered to be stuck fermentation if the same figure is recorded over a period of two weeks or more.

There are many possible causes of this frustrating state of affairs, most of which can be avoided by careful management of the fermentation. However, the following list may help winemakers to recognise and avoid the adverse conditions which might induce a fermentation to cease prematurely.

CAUSES

(a) Inadequate Temperature Control

Fermenting the must at temperatures of over 80°F. (26.7°C.) is likely to cause death of the yeast cells, which then descend to the bottom of the jar, and fermentation ceases. Temperatures below 50°F. cause the yeast ot hibernate, and fermentation to cease.

(b) Poor Yeast Starter

If there is insufficient yeast growth in the starter bottle prior to inoculation of the must, the yeast colony may not be adequate to sustain fermentation to completion. It might be that the yeast used is a poor strain, or that it has been badly stored. More likely is that the winemaker has not made up a sufficiently nutritious medium to promote good growth of yeast in the starter bottle, or has not allowed enough time for the yeast colony to become established.

However, with the use of yeasts, such as 'Formula 67', which have their own nutrients incorporated, this problem rarely occurs. Most other yeasts require making up into nutritious starter bottles (as described in Chapter V, pp. 79–80) at least 48 hours before they are required.

(c) Lack of Nourishment in the Must

Care should be taken to ensure that the must is prepared correctly, and that yeast nutrients are *always* added. This ensures that the yeast is adequately nourished during fermentation, permitting a level of 16–17% alcohol by volume to be reached—or even a little more if required.

(d) Excess Sugar

This is the most common cause of stuck fermentations, usually due to too much sugar being added to the original must. The commencing S.G. of 7 pints (4 litres) should never exceed 1.120, or problems will result.

Feeding in the extra sugar syrup should not begin until the S.G. has dropped to 1.000 or below (before each addition). Care must be taken towards the end of the secondary fermentation, when yeast activity is so slow that only small additions of sugar syrup can be made (maybe only 1 or 2 tablespoonsful at a time), since the alcohol tolerance of the yeast is nearing its limit at this stage.

(e) Excessive Sulphiting

Care should be taken not to use more than one Campden tablet or 5 ml. of sulphite solution when preparing the must, or yeast growth will be severely inhibited, if not stopped altogether.

REMEDIES FOR STUCK FERMENTATIONS

Stuck fermentations are notoriously difficult to restart in

most cases, but there are various simple remedies that may be tried before resorting to the 'doubling up' method. It must be noted that it is normally useless to add a fresh yeast starter direct to the wine, since it will have no resistance to the toxic effect of the alcohol already produced in the wine, and fermentation will not restart.

(a) Aeration

The wine should be splashed through a large funnel from one jar to another a few times, to aerate it. The oxygen absorbed by the wine during this process may induce the yeast to begin to multiply once more, and fermentation may restart.

(b) Addition of Nutrients

One teaspoonful of yeast nutrient, a little yeast energiser, and a 3 mg. vitamin B tablet could increase the nourishment of the yeast sufficiently to stimulate its revival.

(c) Change of Temperature

If the wine has obviously been overheated, the jar should be moved to a cooler place. Sufficient live yeast cells might have survived to establish a new colony, though this is unlikely. In a wine that has been fermenting at too low a temperature, say 50°F. (10°C.), most of the yeast cells will have become dormant, in which case the act of moving the jar to a warmer place may stimulate the yeast cells into action once more.

(d) Dilution

By the addition of water, the alcohol and excess sugar present become diluted, thus reducing their growth-inhibiting influence, and the yeast has a chance of reviving. This means, however, that there will be little or no room left in the jar for further additions of sugar syrup, should the fermentation restart.

(e) Doubling-up Method

If simpler remedies fail, then the following procedure may be followed. A fresh starter bottle should be prepared, and when fermenting vigorously it should be put into a sterile jar together with a pint (568 ml.) of the stuck wine, the neck of the jar then being covered with a tissue or a plug of cotton wool. After a few days in a warm temperature (70°F., 21°C.), when fermentation is strongly established, another pint (568 ml.) of the stuck wine is added. When this in turn is fermenting well, a further 2 pints (1.14 litres) of the wine is added, and when this half gallon (2.25 litres) is going strongly it may be mixed with the remaining near half gallon of the original wine. The must should then ferment out as usual— one hopes!

If the wine shows reluctance to ferment well, it may be advisable to add only 1 pint (568 ml.) at a time instead of doubling-up.

A wine which has stuck at a fairly high specific gravity should re-ferment quite well because the alcohol content will not be so great as to inhibit unduly the growth of the yeast. If, however, the S.G. is down to say 1.025, and a dry wine is desired, it is extremely difficult to persuade it to ferment out because of the inhibiting effect of the high alcohol content already present. It may, therefore, be necessary to accept the wine as a sweet one.

If it is obvious that too much sugar has inadvertently been used in the preparation of the must, then it is essential to dilute with water before attempting refermentation, to prevent death of the fresh yeast cells due to the excessively high osmotic pressure.

Once fermentation of a stuck wine has been re-established, the air-lock should be replaced and fermentation conducted as usual. Sugar syrup additions may be made as required if the fermentation is sufficiently sound.

(f) Mixing with Another Fermenting Wine

This method of restarting a fermentation is very useful if fresh ingredients are available. Where possible, make up another must using the same flavour ingredients as in the stuck wine, and when it is fermenting strongly (after about a week) mix the two together. The two jars of wine so obtained should ferment out well, and sugar additions may be made at intervals following the usual procedures.

If the same flavour ingredients are not available, any other strongly fermenting wine of a similar type will suffice.

(2) Hazes

All wines should, if prepared correctly, clear on their own, given time. This may take a few days, weeks or months, and it is preferable to allow clearing to occur naturally rather than resort to fining or filtering methods, most of which affect the taste and chemical balance of a wine.

Drastically lowering the temperature of wine usually encourages it to clear more rapidly, and this may be brought about by placing it in the refrigerator for a few days, and racking immediately after removal.

If a wine stubbornly refuses to clear, and yet no sediment is being deposited, then the haze is most likely due to something other than yeast. The types of hazes that might be encountered, and how to deal with them, are described below.

(a) Pectin Haze

A pectin haze can, of course, always be prevented by including a pectin-destroying enzyme in the preparation of a must that contains *any* fruit or vegetables. If, however, this has been overlooked, it is a simple matter to test a small sample of the wine to ascertain if pectin is in fact present.

One part (say 5 ml.) of wine is mixed with three to four parts (15–20 ml.) of methylated spirits in a glass. If a flocculent, gelatinous precipitate forms, then pectin is present.

If pectin is found to be the cause of the haze, it is easily removed from the wine by addition of one of the pectin-destroying enzymes—preferably a liquid one such as Pectolase, since there is much less sediment produced (with consequent loss of wine during racking) than when bran-based enzymes are used.

The required amount of enzyme (refer to the instructions on the bottle or packet) is mixed with a glassful of the wine. This is then added to the bulk, and stirred in thoroughly with the handle of a long wood or plastic spoon. The jar is left for a few days to allow the precipitate to settle, and the wine is carefully racked. An inch (25 mm.) or so of wine and sediment may be left in the bottom of the jar. If loss of this wine is to be prevented, it should be put through a filter paper in a funnel, to strain off the precipitate. Otherwise any loss of volume should be made up with wine of the same type, or with cold water, to ensure that no air-space is left in the jar.

(b) Starch Haze

This may occur in wines made from root vegetables, cereals such as wheat or barley, apples and unripe bananas. It may be prevented by use of a cereal wine yeast (not easily available) or by the addition of a starch-reducing enzyme when the must is prepared. However starch hazes do not occur very frequently even if the above ingredients are used, so that it is not essential to go to these lengths.

If, in a finished wine, a haze is thought to be caused by starch, a simple test may be employed to verify this supposition.

Add a few drops of iodine (*not* the decolourised kind) to a small sample of the wine. If it turns blue, starch is present.

Having ascertained that starch is causing the haze, treatment with a starch-reducing enzyme such as Amylozyme should be undertaken. One $\frac{1}{4}$ oz. (7 gm.) of enzyme should be thoroughly mixed with a little of the wine, and the mixture added to the bulk. If the jar is kept in a warm place for a few days, clarification may be observed. The wine is then carefully racked, and any residue filtered if wished, making sure to top up the jar afterwards.

(c) Metallic Hazes

These should never occur, since no metal should ever come into contact with the wine during its preparation and fermentation. However, if contact has been made at some time with iron, lead, copper, tin or zinc, persistent white or coloured hazes may be formed, and a metallic taste be detectable. The haze will increase during the maturing process, but this may be arrested by the addition of a little citric acid. The wine is then fined or filtered to remove the haze.

Old-fashioned lead-glazed fermenting vessels may be the cause of a metallic haze, and of course any traces of lead in the wine are quite cumulatively poisonous. If there is any doubt at all as to the suitability of the container, it should not be used.

(d) Oxidation

A wine which becomes badly oxidised will not only turn brown, but will also develop a hazy appearance. Such wines are not worth salvaging, since their flavour and quality are so

112

much impaired. Good winemaking procedure, strictly followed, should prevent this disaster from occurring.

(e) Protein Hazes

A wine that has a haze which is found *not* to be due to any of the preceding problems probably has a protein haze. In this case, fining or filtering will be necessary in order to remove it.

Old-fashioned fining agents such as egg white, ox blood, casein or isinglass, gelatine and milk should be avoided, since they may cause a variety of other problems. There are many brands of specific wine finings on the market, most of which are acceptable, but they do present a slight problem in that they remove tannin from the wine in the process of clearing it. Therefore it is wise to add a little tea or grape tannin at the same time as the finings to prevent loss of quality. Care must be taken not to exceed the recommended dose of finings, or the wine may not in fact clear.

The most widely used and recommended fining agent is Bentonite (an hydrated aluminium silicate) which is a powdered clay having the surprising property of being able to combine with the protein particles in the wine and precipitate them to the bottom of the jar, without affecting the chemical balance or flavour of the wine. The bentonite has to be made into a suspension with a little water or wine, and left for 24 hours for the particles of clay to absorb liquid and swell. Making the suspension is best done with a whisk or liquidiser, or by pounding the mixture in a bottle by shaking vigorously. After 24 hours the mixture is added to the wine and mixed thoroughly. The jar should be agitated frequently over a period of a few hours and then left for the sediment to settle for a few days. Careful racking should follow and the loss in volume made good with water or wine of a similar type. It is unsatisfactory to try to rescue the wine from the residue left in the jar, as it will almost completely clog up filter papers.

Personal experience has shown that bentonite may very occasionally refuse to clear a wine. Only then is it necessary to resort to ordinary wine-finings, which will usually clear such wines successfully.

Mechanical filters may be used, but obviously entail additional expense. Also they do tend adversely to affect the quality of the wine, and in particular those filters that use powders often impart a 'filter pad' flavour. Filtered wines should be rested for a few weeks or months in the hope that their quality will be restored.

Finally, it is worth noting that the use of black bananas (boiled or pressure cooked in water) in the preparation of the must, helps to speed up clarification of the wine during maturation. I have applied this interesting property to the problem of dealing with stubborn hazes in maturing wines. My method is to boil or pressure cook 1 lb. (0.45 kilo) of peeled black bananas in, say, a pint (0.6 litre) of water, strain off the juice and add 3–4 fl. oz. (85–114 ml.) to each gallon of hazy wine. A little pectin destroying enzyme is added at the same time, to destroy any pectin released into the banana juice during cooking. The wine and banana juice is thoroughly blended, and the jar is then set aside for a day or two until clarification is complete. This method is not guaranteed to work with *all* hazy wines, but I have found it very successful in the great majority of cases.

Using banana juice has a distinct advantage over the use of most proprietary finings or filters, in that tannin is not removed from the wine during the process, and a little extra body is added to the wine while the flavour is hardly affected. This method is certainly well worth trying out.

(3) POOR FLAVOURS

The following conditions are among some of the more frequent causes of the development of poor flavours in wine.

(a) *Poor Yeast*

An inferior yeast, such as bakers or brewers yeast may have-been used for the ferementation, which may impart, a bread like or beery flavour to the wine. A good wine yeast will prevent this occurrence.

(b) *Prolonged Contact with Decaying Lees*

Wine left standing on the lees long after fermentation has ceased, will almost certainly develop off flavours due to the production of fusel oils, caused by the breakdown of dead yeast cells and decaying vegetable or fruit pulp debris (autolysis). A musty, unpalatable wine results, which, even if

114

racked and sulphited, will not improve and is probably fit only for discarding. Again, good technique would not allow this to happen, since regular racking, particularly in the early stages of maturation, would remove the offending sediment before spoilage could occur.

(c) Oxidation

Oxidation should not occur with proper care and attention, but occasionally it does happen by accident. The air-lock in the storage jar may become dry, or the cork used to seal the jar may be of poor quality or be split, so that excess air is allowed in during maturation. If the wine is racked carelessly, splashing it into the receiving jar, or if the jar is not topped up adequately after racking, oxidation may occur. Failure to sulphite the wine after the first two rackings will also encourage oxidation.

An oxidised wine develops a brown colour and a sherry-like flavour and bouquet. If the process is advanced, the flavour becomes musty and a sharp, bitter, unpleasant taste develops due to undesirable chemical reactions having taken place. A very oxidised wine is completely unacceptable for normal drinking, and may only have limited use for cooking.

If a wine showing a tendency to oxidise is discovered soon enough, and if the basic ingredients lend themselves to it, an acceptable sherry-type wine may result. The addition of 1 or 2 Campden tablets or 5–10 ml. of stock sulphite solution will prevent further oxidation. It will be necessary to rest the wine afterwards for a few weeks or months before drinking, so that the residual sulphite is not too obvious to the palate.

Red wines present a slight problem here, because the addition of sulphite bleaches out some of their colour, but if left for a few weeks the deep red hue will return as the effect of the sulphite wears off. Some winemakers prefer to use some other antioxidant, such as vitamin C, which does not de-colourise the wine. However the antioxidant properties of vitamin C are short-lived, so that this is of little use for long-term storage.

(d) Lack of Acid

Wines lacking acidity tend to develop medicinal flavours and are insipid to taste. If the flavour is not affected too badly,

115

additions of small amounts of citric acid (or tartaric, malic and citric acid mixture) may be made. The wine should be tasted after each addition until the balance is found to be restored. Alternatively the wine may be blended with one that is over-acid, experimenting with the proportions of each until the right balance is obtained.

(e) Excess Acid

In the case of over-acidity, a robust, full-bodied wine may be diluted a little with water, which may reduce the acidity to an acceptable level. Addition of sugar syrup to a dry or medium wine will to some extent mask the excess acidity, but will naturally alter the character of the wine. However it is worth sacrificing a little of the quality in order to render the wine drinkable. Glycerine, added at the rate of four to six tablespoons per gallon, can also be used to mask excessive acidity.

Blending with an acid-deficient wine can be undertaken.

Alternatively it is possible to remove the excess acid by successive small additions of precipitated chalk or potassium carbonate (obtainable from chemists). Add one teaspoonful to the gallon, mix thoroughly and taste a day or two later. Repeat the procedure, but using only $\frac{1}{2}$ teaspoonful at a time until the correct balance is restored. Time must be allowed for the precipitate formed to settle to the bottom of the jar so that the clear wine may be racked off into a fresh jar, from where it may be bottled. The acidity may be obtained by titration and consequent amounts of chalk or potassium carbonate to reduce it may be determined (see Chapter V, p. 72).

It is wise to remember that young wines have a tendency to be over-acid in any event, and that the normal processes during maturation may well reduce the acidity to acceptable proportions. Hence be very wary of diagnosing over-acidity in wines that have not fully matured.

(f) Lack of Tannin

A wine deficient in tannin tends to be insipid and characterless to the palate, lacking zest and that slight astringency so vital to a good wine. Usually the remedy for this fault is to blend the wine with one that is too harsh and astringent, such as an elderberry wine made from a poor crop. Again, experimentation with varying proportions should be undertaken to produce the best result.

Tannin, in the form of grape tannin or tea, may be added to the wine, but in my experience this tends to cause the wine to become cloudy, and difficulty may be encountered in attempting to clear it again.

(g) Excess Tannin

Excess tannin in a wine gives it a very harsh, astringent quality detectable by a drying effect on the roof of the mouth, gums and teeth.

Some of the tannin may be removed by experimental additions of wine finings, which cause it to precipitate. It is wise to experiment with a sample of about 1 pint or $\frac{1}{2}$ litre, adding a small amount of finings, mixing thoroughly and tasting 24 hours later, repeating the procedure until the balance is restored. The quantity of finings required for the whole gallon may then be calculated.

Addition of sugar syrup or glycerine, as for an over-acid wine, will to some extent mask the astrigency, although the overall balance of the wine will be upset, as indicated previously. However this is the simplest and quickest way of rendering the wine acceptable to the not over-critical palate.

Blending with a wine lacking in tannin may produce an acceptable result.

(h) Low Alcohol Content

Wines containing less than about 8% alcohol by volume (probably due to a stuck fermentation) do not adequately stimulate the palate, tasting rather more like a cordial. More important than this is the fact that wines of low alcohol content do not have good keeping qualities, being prone to bacterial infections. They must either be consumed when young, or preferably blended with stronger wines or fortified.

(i) Excess Alcohol

Many winemakers have one (erroneous) objective in mind and that is to obtain the highest possible alcohol content in their wines, regardless of the wine type. If the alcohol is predominant, then the wine is unbalanced, and can even be unpleasant. For example, a dry table wine would not be expected to contain 16% alcohol by volume, which would render it akin to an aperitif whilst lacking the other characteristics essential to this type of wine.

Therefore it is desirable to exercise control over the initial sugar content used in the must by deciding beforehand what type of wine is to be made, and using Table 1 (p.59) as already described, to calculate the necessary sugar syrup additions.

(*j*) *Filter Pad Flavour*

This is often noticeable after filtration through mechanical filters (using filter powders) or asbestos pulp. It is almost impossible to describe this off-flavour—a slight earthy, mustiness which will usually eventually disappear on longer maturation.

(*k*) *Diseases*

Some of the diseases which occur in wines may impart off-flavours to them. These are discussed in the appropriate sections below.

DISEASES
(1) Acetification

In most cases this is caused by bacteria (*Mycoderma aceti.* and related organisms, though some film yeasts may have the same disastrous effects. The bacteria attack the alcohol in a wine and convert it to acetic acid, the principal component of vinegar, which is immediately detectable by smell and taste) Such a wine can only be relegated to the kitchen, for use in salad dressings and so forth, or be poured down the sink.

Use of unsound fruit may have been responsible for the introduction of these bacteria to the must in the first place. Airborne spores and fruit flies are often agents of infection, so it must be ensured that they can have no access to fermenting wines, by keeping buckets well covered and air-locks topped up with sulphite solution. The presence of sulphite in the air-lock and the act of ensuring that all vessels containing maturing wine are literally full to the bung will effectively prevent spoilage. The temperature of the wine should never be more than 80°F. (26.7°C.), since *Mycoderma aceti* thrives above this level. As in most cases, prevention is better than cure.

If acetification occurs during fermentation, two Campden tablets or 10 ml. stock strong sulphite solution should be added to the must to kill the bacteria. After 24 hours, when the effect of the sulphite will have worn off sufficiently, fermentation may be re-started by the doubling up method used for stuck fermentations. Most of the acetic acid will be driven off during fermentation, and the wine may be saved.

Acetification of a finished wine can rarely be treated successfully, unless discovered in its very early stages, when the addition of two Campden tablets or their equivalent will prevent further spoilage.

(2) Flowers of Wine

This disease is caused by film yeasts called *Candida mycoderma*, and it may occasionally occur in finished wines. Small white flecks or patches develop on the surface of the still wine, gradually extending until the surface is completely covered with a whitish folded skin. If this skin is broken up, it will sink to the bottom of the jar, but another will form.

The alcohol in the wine is converted into water and carbon dioxide over a period of a few months. Adequate sulphiting and keeping all vessels air-tight and well topped up should prevent this disease occurring.

As soon as this infection is detected, treat it with two Campden tablets or 10 ml. stock sulphite solution. Leave it for a few days so that the white particles have time to settle to the bottom of the jar, and then rack the wine into a sterile jar. Top up with water, and examine the wine every few weeks in case re-infection should occur.

(3) Ropiness

Ropiness is caused by a species of lactic acid bacteria that produces, a thick, oily appearance in the wine. If the disease is advanced, the wine pours like white of egg, or even treacle, but fortunately the flavour and alcohol content are practically unaffected. Treatment with two Campden tablets or 10 ml. stock sulphite solution, with vigorous stirring to break up the chains of bacteria, will kill the infection. After 24 hours the wine should be racked or filtered through filter paper (to remove any deposit) into a sterile jar, and then rested for a few weeks before drinking.

(4) Tourne Disease

Another species of lactic acid bacteria causes this disorder, the characteristic sympton of which is a silky sheen observed in the wine when it is swirled against a strong light. Once more, eliminating access of air to the wine and sulphiting it will prevent this disease occurring.

Off-flavours develop if the disease is allowed to become advanced, but in the early stages it may be successfully treated with two Campden tablets or 10 ml. stock sulphite solution.

(5) Malolactic Fermentation

This disease (which is of more frequent occurrence than are the other four) is caused by yet another species of lactic acid bacteria. It is found mainly in wines made from fruit containing malic acid, but may be noticed in other wines to which malic acid has been added as part of the acid mixture. The malic acid in the wine becomes converted into (the less acidic) lactic acid with the production of carbon dioxide. The result is an absolutely clear wine which is less acidic than before, and is sparkling due to the dissolved carbon dioxide.

In a dry wine this malolactic fermentation usually results in an improvement of quality, and a beautiful sparkling wine can be produced without the fuss normally entailed in making a wine of this type. However if it occurs in a sweet wine, the sugar is attacked and converted into rather unpleasant-tasting by-products, in which case the wine should be treated early with the usual dose of two Campden tablets or 10 ml. of stock sulphite solution to kill the bacteria and prevent the development of undesirable off-flavours.

A sparkling dry wine containing this disease may be bottled in champagne-type bottles with the corks wired down. It should not be stored for long, though, or the acidity may be reduced below the desired level.

Happily, the diseases described in this chapter do not often occur if proper care and attention are given to the wine at all times during its production.

120

CHAPTER VIII

Serving Wine

HAVING spent much time preparing and maturing one's wines it is well worth giving considerable attention to the serving of them. Winemakers are usually very proud of most of their products and wish to do them justice by serving them correctly, particularly on special occasions. In this chapter, I hope to give a few helpful suggestions.

Wines certainly look their best when presented in the correct type of bottle—white and rosé mainly in clear glass, but occasionally in the slender brown or green Hock or Reisling type bottle; red (and rosé) in coloured bottles to preserve the colour of the wine. If bottles are attractively and informatively labelled and sealed with a good cork and a foil or plastic capsule, the effect is aesthetically very pleasing. (Squash, spirit or beer bottles do not look the part and are preferably avoided unless they are absolutely necessary.) Decanters are very useful but care must be taken not to leave wine in them for more than a day or two if the stoppers are not airtight. Spoilage, due to oxidation, can occur quite quickly.

At all times, proper wine glasses should be used, preferably clear, as opposed to coloured glass so that the colour and clarity of the wine may be displayed to best advantage. Aperitifs, liqueurs and fortified wines are normally served in smaller glasses than those used for table and dessert wines. This is because they have a much higher alcohol content than the latter types and therefore are consumed in smaller quantities.

When arranging a dinner party, some thought should be given beforehand to the types of wine that will be required before and throughout the meal.

Aperitifs are wines which are traditionally served before a meal, to stimulate the appetite. These should be served chilled and bottles may be placed in the refrigerator for a few hours before they are required. Alternatively, they may be stored at room temperature and the wine served with ice.

White table wines, sparkling and rosé wines should be chilled before serving. Such wines are much improved by this treatment, being 'crisper' than when consumed at room temperature. Traditionally, they are drunk with delicate flavoured foods such as hors d'oeuvres, salads, fish, shellfish, or poultry so that neither the food nor the wine is overpowered.

Red table wines should be brought into room temperature a few hours before they are required and the cork should be drawn one hour before serving to allow the wine to 'breathe'. The bouquet of red wines is more pronounced when the wine is prepared in this way. These wines complement red meat, game or any strongly flavoured dish.

Dessert wines are rich and sweet and are meant to be drunk with the sweet course. White dessert wines are probably best served slightly chilled and the red at room temperature, as for table wines.

After-dinner wines such as ports, sweet sherries and liqueurs are normally served at room temperature, the latter usually being consumed with coffee.

The guide lines given above refer to the traditional types of wines to serve with the different courses of a meal. These days however, it is generally accepted that one may drink what one prefers. For example, many people prefer white table wine to red, in which case they may be offered a white wine with a red meat or strongly flavoured dish. If a person wishes to have a Sauternes with fish or poultry, this is acceptable since the French occasionally serve such a wine with this type of food.

Most winemakers produce a large proportion of social wines which are generally stronger flavoured and more alcoholic than table wines but less full-bodied and rich than dessert wines. Such wines are suitable for casual drinking with friends, at parties or just as a pleasant, relaxing beverage in the evening when the day's work is done. As a general rule, the white wines should be chilled and the red served at room temperature, but for social wines this is not unduly important. Winemakers normally store their maturing wines in a fairly cool place so that if wine is required in a hurry, such as when friends call unexpectedly, it will have to be served at the temperature dictated by that of the winery. I would imagine that complaints are rare!

As an amateur winemaker, one can contemplate throwing parties much more frequently than if one had to provide commercial wines and spirits. Our own experience has been that friends tend to become somewhat embarassed by frequent party invitations which they cannot always return, so they suggest that *they* provide the food since we have plentiful supplies of cheap wine. Instead of a 'bottle' party, we have a 'food' party, everyone bringing something different and interesting. It works very well.

It is a wonderful feeling to be able to supply suitable wines for any occasion. The only regret, suffered by many amateurs, is that their really superb wines tend to disappear at an alarming rate! This is a very good reason for producing wine in bulk, such as three, five or ten gallon batches, when one has found a particularly reliable recipe.

There are a couple of final points which I feel should be mentioned. People sometimes ask whether one can drink a number of *different* wines without ill-effects. The answer, is 'yes', as long as the quantities consumed are in moderation as with any form of alcoholic beverage. Problems usually only arise when spirits, beer and wine are drunk during a social occasion. The old adage, 'the grain and the grape do not mix', is very wise!

Occasionally, without realising it, a person may drink a homemade wine prepared from some fruit or flower to which they are allergic. If this should occur, then ill-effects might be suffered by they are usually of a transitory nature. Such wines obviously should be avoided in the future.

CHAPTER IX

Winemaking Organisations
and Sources of Information

IN the last twenty years, the popularity of amateur wine-making has increased tremendously. In 1954 a few interested people got together and formed wine circles here and there, to exchange information and increase their knowledge. Enthusiasm spread like ripples on a pool until now there are over a thousand clubs, scattered about the British Isles. Wherever one lives there is likely to be a wine circle not too far away. They usually meet regularly, once a month or once a fortnight and have a varied programme of talks, demonstrations, films, competitions and social events. Each meeting is a very sociable occasion as well as usually being instructive for beginners and more advanced winemakers alike. It is very stimulating to meet other winemakers, taste their wines and learn how they were produced; to enter competitions and maybe win an award and to enjoy the shared interest and camaraderie which invariably exists. The local library should be able to supply the name and address of the secretary of the nearest wine circle.

In most areas of the country, wine circles belong to a regional Federation of Amateur Winemakers. Each Federation holds an annual show or festival, usually a weekend event comprising the competition itself, talks, discussions and a dance on the Saturday evening. The show is most often an 'open' competition, so that winemakers who do not belong to member circles may enter the various wine, beer or cookery classes. The larger Federation shows may have twenty or thirty or forty classes, the majority of which are for different types of wines and competition is very keen.

Attending and exhibiting in Federation shows is a very exciting and interesting way of spending the occasional weekend. Friendships are struck and renewed each year, and much useful advice and information may be obtained by talking to the judges of the show classes and to other experienced winemakers with whom one comes into contact.

The judges at these shows are usually National Judges and/or Federation judges who are trained to a high standard within their organisation. National Judges are members of The Amateur Winemakers National Guild of Judges (A.W.N.G.J.).

To become a National Judge, one must have a sound knowledge of winemaking practice and be well acquainted with winetasting and judging techniques. Examinations are held each year by the Guild of Judges and the standard required to become a member is very high. There are now almost two hundred National Judges. For those winemakers who are interested in becoming a member of the A.W.N.G.J., application should be made to the Chief Examiner, S. W. Andrews, Esq., 6 Tamworth Road, Hertford.

The National Association of Wine and Beermakers (N.A.W.B.), is an organisation to which individuals, wine circles and Federations may belong. It exists to further interest in wine and beermaking nationwide. It holds an annual conference and show, generally known as 'The National', one weekend near Easter-time. A different venue is chosen each year, but they are held more often in the south than in the north of the country, since there is a greater concentration of winemaking activity in the south.

The National is *the* great event in a winemakers diary. It is a very large show, the number of entries having risen enormously over the last few years to around 4,000 bottles. In its present form, there are 13 'open' classes (including wine, beer, cookery and bottle-label design) in which anyone may exhibit, whether or not they are a member of the N.A.W.B. Members classes number 26 in all, four of which are for wine-circle or Federation entries.

All judging of wines and beers is done by National Judges and it is of great interest to discuss one's entries with the judges concerned at the 'Judges at the Bar' session on the Saturday afternoon. Much can be learnt from such discussion!

Awards won at the National are much prized possessions and one always hopes that a silver trophy may be gained some day. During the conference weekend there are talks and discussions and the Annual General Meeting of the N.A.W.B. There is a buffet dance on the Saturday night which is always a very sociable and enjoyable occasion, particularly when one may take one's own wines to drink.

Occasionally, the National is held in a place where resident accommodation is available, such as at Nottingham University in 1976. This sort of arrangement is very welcome when it is possible since a much more friendly atmosphere is created by everyone being 'under one roof' rather than scattered about in different hotels.

All in all, the National is well worth attending, particularly if one is exhibiting.

The N.A.W.B. produce a quarterly newsletter for members and they are very keen to have communication with as many winemakers as possible. News and views are exchanged through this medium.

The Amateur Winemaker is a very helpful and interesting monthly magazine obtainable through newsagents or from The Amateur Winemaker Publications Ltd., South St. Andover, Hants. It was first published in 1957 and now has a very wide circulation. It contains articles of varied interest written by notable winemakers and beer experts, recipes for wine, beer and cookery, handy tips and hints and a selection of readers' problems and their solutions. This magazine has been a great asset to winemakers over the years, keeping them abreast of modern trends.

In most areas of the country the local Adult Association includes a winemaking course in its programme. These classes are extremely helpful, particularly to the beginner, but many people who have been winemaking for some years, can benefit from the expert advice and practical demonstrations. I began my own winemaking 'career' by attending evening classes 11 years ago and our local wine circle was formed in that year by our lecturer and many of her very interested pupils. We now have two National Judges and two potential National Judges among our members. From small beginnings, great interest and enthusiasm has grown and a thriving club exists to prove it.

There are many books available, mostly in paperback,

which will assist winemakers. The Amateur Winemaker Publications Ltd., publish over 50 titles, many of which are specialised in certain aspects of our craft, such as making sparkling wines, mead, cider and woodwork for winemakers. A comprehensive list of books may be found in each copy of *The Amateur Winemaker* or may be obtained by writing to the publishers—The Amateur Winemaker Publications Ltd., at the address mentioned previously.

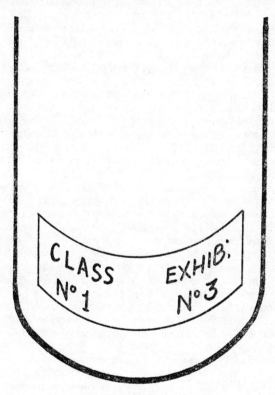

Fig. 12
Example of bottle labelling for show purposes

CHAPTER X

Exhibiting Wine

WHETHER entering wines in small club competitions or in the larger shows mentioned in the last chapter, there are certain basic rules to which one must pay close attention. Copies of these rules are usually available from the wine circle committee or, in the case of the Federation and National shows, the rules are clearly printed in the schedule.

It is very important to ensure that the wines being entered fit the description of the appropriate class. For example, in a 'Dry table wine' class, it is pointless to enter a wine which contains residual sugar as it will be marked well down or disqualified by the judge. Similarly, a sweet *social* wine would not be acceptable in a dessert wine class. It is well worth conducting a very objective tasting session in the winery beforehand, making notes as to which wines are suitable for the classes available.

Check the schedule to find out whether rosé wines are allowed in the red wine classes and tawny wines in the white wine classes. Rules on these points do vary from show to show.

All wines should be of good quality, brilliantly clear, stable and free of floaters or sediment.

If wines are to be blended to produce the type of wine required, this should be done a few weeks before the show to allow time for a complete marrying of the flavours. Blending occasionally causes fermentation to recommence or hazes to appear in what were perfectly clear wines previously. Should either happen, filtering through one of the mechanical filters available may be necessary to render the wine suitable for exhibiting.

Occasionally a wine may require some sweetening. If so, then this should be done well in advance to ensure complete homogeneity. Unfortunately this may cause refermentation, but if one adds a little sulphite at the time of sweetening, it may be prevented.

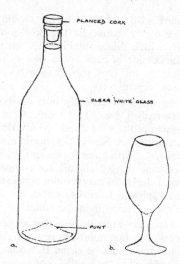

FLANGED CORK

CLEAR 'WHITE' GLASS

PUNT

a.   b.

Fig. 11   Type of bottle   Copita for
for Exhibiting   Judging

For competition purposes, wine bottles should be clear colourless, punted bottles of approximately 26 fl. oz. capacity. Ascertain from the rules whether deep or shallow punted bottles or both, are allowed. The bottle in most common use is the French Sauternes type which has a shallow punt. There must be no external markings on the bottle which could identify the exhibitor. (Many wine bottles have embossed letters, figures or even words on the outside).

Great care should be taken of competition bottles to ensure that they remain scratch-free and clean. To this end, it is useful to store them (when empty) upside down in a sectioned wine carton obtainable from off-licences. If wished, a little dilute sulphite solution may be poured into each bottle, which should then be firmly corked. This procedure would prevent any mould formation during storage.

Clean and sterilise all bottles just before they are required, using Domestos or Chempro S.D.P. (as described in Chapter V). The outside of the bottles should not be ignored in this respect.

129

Thorough rinsing with plenty of water should follow, to remove all trace of the chemicals. The bottles may then be rinsed out with a little dilute sulphite solution followed by cold water. The outside of each bottle should be dried and polished thoroughly and they should then be stood upside down to drain for a few minutes.

Wine must be siphoned carefully into the bottles to the required level (usually $\frac{1}{2}$–$\frac{3}{4}$ in., 13–19 mm.) from the base of the cork. Splashing of the wine should be avoided to prevent undue exposure to the air. New corks should always be used and may be moistened with water for easier application. Most major shows demand flanged all-cork (or composition cork) stoppers but local club rules may require plastic topped corks to be used. Rules applying to corks must be obeyed or entries may be disqualified, certainly in the National.

Corks are of such poor quality now that judges do not pay too much attention to this point but one should choose the best possible and they must be *clean*. If labels are supplied, these should be applied to the bottle in the correct position as stated in the rules. They should be placed midway between the seams of the bottle and a set distance from the base. (See Figure 12). A label is supplied for each entry and unless requested to do so, one should never write on them. The labels normally have printed on them the 'class number' and the 'exhibitors number' and possibly the 'class description,' (e.g. White Dessert). Sometimes, one is asked to write the main ingredient of the wine on the label, in which case it should be done as neatly as possible.

After a final polish with a dry cloth, the bottles should be wrapped in tissue-paper or paper serviettes (to prevent finger-marks) and stored in cool conditions until the show.

Bottling wines a few weeks before a show, allows them time to recover from any 'bottle sickness' which is a temporary after-effect of the bottling process. This is due to aeration of the wine and tends to leave it tasting rather flat and uninteresting. Its former quality is usually regained, given time.

When presenting one's entries at the show, bottles should be handled by the top of the neck and the base of the bottle to avoid unsightly fingerprints spoiling the appearance.

For small club or inter-club competitions, when only one bottle may be required, the same care should be taken in the preparation of the exhibit.

A FEW POINTS ABOUT THE JUDGING OF WINE
Wines are awarded points under four headings:

(1) Presentation
This is marked out of two. Part of a mark may be lost for each of the following: if the bottle or cork is dirty, the label is incorrectly applied, or the level of the wine is too high or too low. A perfectly presented bottle will gain full marks.

(2) Clarity
This is marked out of four. The wine is held up to the light to enable the judge to assess the clarity properly. Marks will be lost for floaters or sediment. A hazy wine will be marked well down. A brilliantly clear wine, containing no foreign matter, will receive full marks.

(3) Bouquet
This is marked out of four. The cork is removed and the bouquet assessed in bottle before pouring out a small sample into a copita (see Figure 11b.) The bouquet is then assessed in the glass. A wine with a poor, unappetising bouquet or one which has very little bouquet, will lose valuable marks. The bouquet should be pleasant and vinous and be appropriate in its strength and character to the particular class of wine. Full marks will then be awarded.

(4) Colour, Flavour, Balance and Quality
This is the most important part of the judging and marks are awarded out of 20. The colour is assessed and should be appropriate to the wine class. The wine is then tasted—it is thoroughly 'chewed' so that it comes into contact with all parts of the palate. It is then spat out. The flavour, balance and quality are judged by the total effect on the palate. (Sweetness is detected on the tip of the tongue, tannin around the gums and cheeks, acid along the sides of the tongue and alcohol just inside the lips, at the back of the tongue and

the rear palate). Any imbalances and the presence of off-flavours will cause loss of marks. The actual mark awarded is not important as it is only relative to those marks given to other wines. Well balanced wines will be awarded relatively high marks.

The wines gaining the highest marks in the last section are brought forward for the final tasting and appreciation and the awarding of 1st., 2nd. and 3rd. prizes etc. Should there be a tie between any of the wines, the marks gained in the other three sections are taken into account in order to separate them. Awards are given according to the show regulations, unless the class is generally poor. In such a case, the judge may withold awards at his own discretion. Occasionally, extra awards may be given in a class of exceptionally high standard.

Judges in small club competitions should try to judge by these nationally accepted rules and standards. In particular, they must attempt not to be distracted by personal preferences as regards flavour and bouquet.

Further detailed information on judging may be found in the official Judges handbook, *Judging Homemade Wine and Beers*, mentioned previously and in the more detailed "Be A Wine Judge" by S. W. Andrews (from the Amateur Wine-maker Publications Ltd.)

BIBLIOGRAPHY

Woodwork for Winemakers
C. J. Dart and D. A. Smith

How to Make Wines with a Sparkle
J. Restall and D. Hebbs

Progressive Winemaking
P. Duncan and B. Acton

Judging Homemade Wines and Beers
Published by the Amateur Winemakers Guild of Judges
(A.W.N.G.J.)

The Amateur Winemaker
Published by The Amateur Winemaker Publications Ltd.

WINEMAKING SUPPLIERS—MAIL ORDER

Beer, Wine and Liqueur Making, 1 Park Road, New Malden,
Surrey.

Rogers (Mead) Ltd., Shirlett, Broseley, Salop. TF12 5BH.

Semplex Home Brews Ltd., Old Hall Works, Stuart Road,
Birkenhead.

S. J. Buckley, West End Winemakers Stores, 198 Dunstable
Road, Luton, Beds.

W. R. Loftus Ltd., 1–3 Charlotte Street, London W1P 1HD.

Hidalgo, 81 Ledbury Road, London W11.

APPENDIX

RECIPES

ALL recipes in this section have been tried and tested by me personally or by eminent winemakers of my acquaintance. A number of them have produced prizewinning wines with awards gained at local, Federation and National level.

Each recipe is for 1 gallon (4.5 litres) of wine, but if bulk production is required, all quantities (with the exception of the yeast) may be increased proportionately.

Chapters V and VI should be read and thoroughly understood before the recipes are attempted. This will ensure that correct procedures are employed and it saves constant repetition in the recipes.

Except where otherwise stated, the preparation of the must always follows the 7 pint (4 litre) method described in Chapter VI.

IMPORTANT POINTS TO REMEMBER

(1) Do not forget to allow for the volume of the *natural fruit juices* extracted during pulp fermentation (see Chapter VI p. 87). This estimated volume must be included in the total of 7 pints (4 litres) of must.

(2) Remember to add up the *total* volume of the different liquids added to the must *before* topping up with water to 7 pints (4 litres) i.e. fruit juices, sugar syrup, tea, yeast starter, banana 'gravy', grape concentrate, boiling water when used etc.

(3) Sugar is always added in the form of *strong sugar syrup* (S.S.S.), the preparation of which is described in Chapter V, p. 54).

(4) The amount of sugar quoted in each recipe is the quantity to be included in the original 7 pints (4 litres) of must. The amount of *extra* S.S.S. to be added in stages during fermentation is calculated after obtaining the S.G. of the origina-7 pints (4 litres) of must. (See Chapter V, p. 61).

(5) The yeast should always be made up into a 'starter' before being introduced into the must. (See Chapter V, p. 78-9).

(6) Where bananas are mentioned, the quantity refers to the fruit only (skins discarded) unless otherwise stated. The

method for the preparation of banana 'gravy' may be found found in Chapter V, p. 52. Approximately $\frac{1}{2}$ pint (284 ml.) of 'gravy' should be prepared from the quantity of bananas given in each recipe.

(7) Remember to take an S.G. reading of the original 7 pints (4 litres) of must *before* any fermentation takes place.

(8) Use Table 1, Chapter V, p. 57 to calculate the necessary extra S.S.S. additions for the particular wine type.

(9) Chapter VI contains all the information necessary about must preparation methods, fermentation and maturation of wines.

APPLE (1)
Wine style—Dry white table wine
4 lb. (1.8 kilos) mixed apples (tart and sweet)
1½ lb. (680 gm.) sugar as S.S.S.
½ lb. (227 gm.) sultanas
1 Campden tablet or 5 ml. strong sulphite solution
Pectin destroying enzyme
3 mg. vitamin B tablet
¼ oz. (7 gm.) citric acid or ⅜ oz. (11 gm.) mixed acids
All purpose or Burgundy yeast starter
Yeast nutrient
Water to make up the total volume to 7 pints (4 litres)

Method

Use Method 2, Chapter VI.

Wash and chop the apples into small chunks adding to 3 pints (1.7 litres) of sulphited water in a sterilised bucket as each piece of fruit is prepared. Mince or liquidise the sultanas and add to the apples together with the pectin destroying enzyme. Cover and leave 24 hours. Next day add all other recipe ingredients, making up the total liquid content to 7 pints (4 litres) with cold tap water. Stir thoroughly, take S.G. reading and subtract from 1.097 or 1.114. Cover and ferment as usual making S.S.S. additions as necessary. Ferment to dryness—S.G. 0.990–1.000 after extra S.S.S. additions.

APPLE (2)
Wine style—Dry white table wine
4 lb. (1.8 kilos) mixed apples
1¼ lb. (567 gm.) sugar as S.S.S.
½ pint (284 ml.) white grape concentrate
1 Campden tablet or 5 ml. strong sulphite solution
Pectin destroying enzyme
3 mg. vitamin B tablet
All purpose or Burgundy yeast starter
Yeast nutrient
Water to make up the volume to 7 pints (4 litres)

Method

Use Method 2, Chapter VI.

Prepare as in Apple (1) adding grape concentrate instead of the sultanas. Mix well, take S.G. reading and subtract from 1.097 or 1.114. The final S.G. should be 0.990–1.000.

APPLE (3)
Wine style—Dry white table wine
By courtesy of Mr. D. G. Turner. Wine of the Year—
Tynemouth W.S. Annual Show 1975 and 1977

5 lb. (2.27 kilos) apples—preferably cookers
1 lb. (454 gm.) over-ripe peeled bananas
¼ can white grape concentrate
1½ lb. (680 gm.) sugar as S.S.S.
Pectin destroying enzyme
Yeast nutrient
All purpose yeast starter
1 Campden tablet or 5 ml. strong sulphite solution

Method

Extract the juice from the apples by a juice extractor or slice thinly (including peel) into water containing the Campden tablet. Peel the bananas, simmer for 20 minutes in 1 pint (568 ml.) of water, strain and add the liquor to the apple. Add the enzyme and allow to stand overnight at 75°F. (24°C.). Add grape concentrate, nutrient and 3 pints (1.7 litres) water. Make up the yeast starter bottle and add at 75°F. (24°C.) with 1 lb. (454 gm.) sugar as syrup. Ferment for four days, strain through a nylon straining bag into a demijohn. Add the remaining sugar as syrup, make up to 1 gallon (4.5 litres) with water and ferment to dryness at 70°–75° F. (21°–24°C.). Allow to stand for two days, rack and store with one Campden tablet.

Drink at four to nine months. Final S.G. should be 0.995. Alcohol content 12%.

APPLE (4)
Wine style—Dry white table wine

2 lb. (0.9 kilo) mixed apples
1 tin white grape concentrate
½ lb. (227 gm.) peeled over-ripe bananas
1 Campden tablet or 5 ml. strong sulphite solution
3 mg. vitamin B tablet
Pectin destroying enzyme
All purpose or Hock type yeast starter
Yeast nutrient
Water to make up the volume to 1 gallon (4.5 litres)

Method

Use Method 2, Chapter VI.

Prepare apples as in Apple (1) and add the grape concentrate and prepared banana 'gravy'. Add pectin destroying enzyme,

137

cover and leave for 24 hours then add all other ingredients, mix thoroughly, taken an S.G. reading and subtract from 1.097 or 1.114. Ferment as usual, making any necessary sugar (S.S.S.) additions and finishing with an S.G. of 0.990–1.000.

APPLE (5)
Wine style—Dry white table wine
4 lb. (1.8 kilos) mixed apples
1 lb. (454 gm.) peeled over-ripe bananas
1¾ lb. (794 gm.) sugar as S.S.S.
Pectin destroying enzyme
¼ oz. (7 gm.) citric acid or ⅜ oz. (11 gm.) acid mixture
3 mg. vitamin B tablet
1 Campden tablet or 5 ml. strong sulphite solution
All purpose or Bordeaux yeast starter
Yeast nutrient
Water to make up the volume to 7 pints (4 litres)

Method

Use Method 2, Chapter VI.

Prepare apples as in Apple (1) and add prepared banana 'gravy' and pectin destroying enzyme when cool. Leave covered for 24 hours then add all other ingredients, mix thoroughly, take an S.G. reading and subtract from 1.097 or 1.114. Ferment as usual making S.S.S. additions as necessary. The final S.G. should be 0.990–1.000.

APPLE (6)
Wine style—Medium dry table or social wine
The use of red grape concentrate will produce a rosé wine.
1 large jar (930 ml.) pure apple juice
½ pint (284 ml.) white or red grape concentrate
1¼ lb. (567 gm.) sugar as S.S.S.
Pectin destroying enzyme
3 mg. vitamin B tablet
All purpose or Bordeaux yeast starter
Yeast nutrient
Water to make up the volume to 7 pints (4 litres)

Method

Put all the ingredients into a clean demijohn and mix thoroughly. Take an S.G. reading and subtract from 1.114. Cover the neck of the jar with a tissue and elastic band. Ferment as usual, making S.S.S. additions as necessary and finish with an S.G. of 1.004–1.010.

APPLE (7)
Wine style—Medium social wine
3 lb. (1.36 kilos) windfall crab-apples
½ lb. (227 gm.) sultanas
1 bottle of Quosh orange and pineapple
1¾ lb. (794 gm.) sugar as S.S.S.
1 Campden tablet or 5 ml. strong sulphite solution
3 mg. vitamin B tablet
Pectin destroying enzyme
All purpose or Bordeaux yeast starter
Yeast nutrient
Water to make up the volume to 7 pints (4 litres)

Method

Use Method 2, Chapter VI.

Prepare the apples and sultanas as in Apple (1). Boil the Quosh cordial for three minutes to remove excess preservative, then add to the bucket. Cover, cool and add pectin destroying enzyme. Leave covered for 24 hours then add all other recipe ingredients, mix well and take an S.G. reading—subtract from 1.131. Ferment as usual, making S.S.S. additions as necessary and finish with an S.G. of 1.006–1.014.

APPLE (8)
Wine style—Sweet social wine
4 lb. (1.8 kilos) windfall crab-apples
1¾ lb. (794 gm.) sugar as S.S.S.
½ lb. (227 gm.) sultanas
1 lb. (454 gm.) peeled over-ripe bananas (plus 2 skins)
1 bottle Quosh orange and pineapple
3 mg. vitamin B tablet
Pectin destroying enzyme
1 Campden tablet or 5 ml. strong sulphite solution
All purpose or Sauternes yeast starter
Yeast nutrient
Water to make up the volume to 7 pints (4 litres)

Method

Use Method 2, Chapter VI.

Prepare apples and sultanas as in Apple (1). Add boiled and cooled Quosh and add prepared banana 'gravy'. Add pectin destroying enzyme, cover and leave 24 hours. Next day add all other ingredients, mix well, take an S.G. reading and subtract from 1.148. Ferment as usual, making S.S.S. additions as necessary. The final S.G. should be 1.020.

139

APPLE (9)
Wine style—Sweet social wine
6 lb. (2.72 kilos) windfall crab-apples
1¾ lb. (794 gm.) sugar as S.S.S.
1½ lb. (680 gm.) peeled over-ripe bananas (plus a few skins)
Pectin destroying enzyme
1 Campden tablet or 5 ml. strong sulphite solution
3 mg. vitamin B tablet
All purpose or Sauternes yeast starter
Yeast nutrient
Water to make up the volume to 7 pints (4 litres)

Method

Use Method 2, Chapter VI.

Prepare the apples as in Apple (1). Add prepared banana gravy' and pectin destroying enzyme. Leave covered for 24 hours then add all other ingredients, mix thoroughly and take and S.G. reading—subtract from 1.148. Ferment as usual making S.S.S. additions as necessary, finishing with an S.G. of 1.020.

N.B. All apple wines can be made to a much higher standard 'if the pure juice is extracted by a press or electric juice extractor before preparing the must. A cleaner, fresher flavour is obtained by utilising the pure juice as opposed to conducting a pulp fermentation. When juice extraction is done, the liquor should be sulphited in the receiving vessel. It is useful to extract the flavour from dried fruit where used, by boiling or pressure cooking, straining off and discarding the pulp and adding the liquor to the apple juice in a clean demijohn. The must is made up as usual and fermentation is conducted following Method 3, Chapter VI.

APRICOT (1)
Wine style—White dry table wine
2 large tins (850 gm. size) apricots
½ lb. (227 gm.) sultanas
1¼ lb. (567 gm.) sugar as S.S.S.
2, 3 mg. vitamin B tablets
¼ cup of tea or 1/30 oz. (1 gm.) grape tannin
Pectin destroying enzyme
1 Campden tablet or 5 ml. strong sulphite solution
All purpose or Burgundy yeast starter
Yeast nutrient
Water to make up the volume to 7 pints (4 litres)

Method

Use Method 1, Chapter VI.

Strain the syrup from the apricots and measure the volume. Empty the fruit and syrup into a sterile bucket and crush. Add the minced or liquidised sultanas and pour over 2 pints (1.14 litres) boiling water. Cool, then add sulphite and pectin destroying enzyme. Cover and leave 24 hours then add all other recipe ingredients, mix well, taken an S.G. reading and subtract from 1.097 or 1.114. Ferment as usual, making S.S.S additions as necessary, finishing with an S.G. of 0.990–1.000.

APRICOT (2)

Wine style—White dry table wine

$\frac{3}{4}$ lb. (340 gm.) dried apricots
$\frac{1}{2}$ lb. (227 gm.) peeled over-ripe bananas
1$\frac{3}{4}$ lb. (794 gm.) sugar as S.S.S.
1 Campden tablet or 5 ml. strong sulphite solution
Pectin destroying enzyme
$\frac{1}{4}$ oz. (7 gm.) citric acid or $\frac{3}{8}$ oz. (11 gm.) acid mixture
3 mg. vitamin B tablet
1 cup strong tea or 1/15 oz. (2 gm.) grape tannin
All purpose or Burgundy yeast starter
Yeast nutrient
Water to make up the volume to 7 pints (4 litres)

Method

Use Method 1, Chapter VI.

Soak the apricots over-night in a measured amount of water, say $\frac{1}{2}$ pint (284 ml.), then mince or liquidise. Put in a sterile bucket and add the prepared banana 'gravy'. Pour over 2 pints (1.14 litres) boiling water, cool, then add sulphite and pectin destroying enzyme. Leave covered for 24 hours then add all other recipe ingredients, mix well, take an S.G. reading and subtract from 1.097 or 1.114. Ferment as usual. making S.S.S. additions as necessary, finishing with an S.G, of 0.990–1.000.

A pleasant medium table wine may be produced by adding a little more S.S.S. to raise the S.G. to about 1.006.

APRICOT (3)

Wine style—Dessert or sweet social wine

By courtesy of Mr. J. Caisley—Vallum Wine Circle
Wine of the Show—Northumbria Federation 1977.

1 lb. (454 gm.) dried apricots
½ lb. (227 gm.) dried figs
½ lb. (227 gm.) dates
½ lb. (227 gm.) sultanas
1 teaspoon citric acid
½ teaspoon tannin or ½ pint (284 ml.) tea
Pectin destroying enzyme
2½ lb. (1.13 kilos) sugar
All purpose yeast starter
Yeast nutrient
Water

Method

Chop up the dried fruits and place with 1½ lb. (680 gm.) of sugar in a bucket. Pour over 4 pints (2.27 litres) boiling water and stir to dissolve the sugar. Cool and add tannin, acid, pectin destroying enzyme, yeast starter and nutrient, and water to make up to 7 pints (4 litres)—approximately 2 pints (1.14 litres). Ferment on the pulp for seven days stirring twice daily, ensuring that the bucket is kept closely covered. Strain into a demijohn and ferment as usual, making 4 oz. (113 gm.) sugar additions (as S.S.S.) each time the S.G. drops to 1,000 or below, finishing with an S.G. of 1.020 with the last addition.

BANANA (1)

Wine style—White dry table wine

5 lb. (2.27 kilos) over-ripe bananas
2 lb. (0.9 kilo) sugar as S.S.S.
3 mg. vitamin B tablet
Pectin destroying enzyme
½ cup of tea or 1/30 oz. (1 gm.) grape tannin
½ oz. (14 gm.) citric acid or ¾ oz. (21 gm.) acid mixture
All purpose or Bordeaux yeast starter
Yeast nutrient
Water to make up the volume to 7 pints (4 litres)

Method

Use Method 3, Chapter VI.

Peel and chop the banana fruit and put in a pressure cooker or pan with two skins and 2–3 pints (1.14–1.7 litres) of water. Simmer in a pan (with a lid) for 20 minutes or pressure cook at 15 lb. (6.8 kilos) pressure for five minutes. Strain off and discard the pulp. Measure the amount of banana liquor remaining, cool and pour into a sterilised demijohn. Add pectin destroying enzyme. (Note that the banana liquor will be grey in colour and may jellify on cooling due to the high pectin content.) Cover the neck of the jar with a tissue and elastic band and leave 24 hours. Then add all other ingredients, mix well, take an S.G. reading and subtract from 1.097 or 1.114. Ferment as usual adding extra S.S.S. as necessary, finishing with an S.G. of 0.990–1.000.

BANANA (2)

Wine style—Sweet white social or dessert wine

5 lb. (2.27 kilos) over-ripe bananas

2¼ lb. (1.02 kilos) sugar as S.S.S.

3 mg. vitamin B tablet

½ cup of tea or 1/30 oz. (1 gm.) grape tannin

Pectin destroying enzyme

1 Campden tablet or 5 ml. strong sulphite solution

¾ oz. (21 gm.) citric acid or 1 oz. (28 gm.) acid mixture

All purpose or Sauternes yeast starter

Yeast nutrient

Water to make up the volume to 7 pints (4 litres)

Method

Use Method 3, Chapter VI.

Prepare the bananas as in Banana (1) using all fruit and *half* the skins. When the liquor is cool measure the amount and pour into a clean demijohn. Add sulphite and pectin destroying enzyme. Leave covered for 24 hours then add all other ingredients, mix well, take S.G. and subtract from 1.148. Ferment as usual making S.S.S. additions as necessary, finishing with an S.G. of 1.020.

BILBERRY (1)
Wine style—Red dry table wine
By courtesy of Mr. T. D. Hodkinson, 1st. Prize¾National 1976, Fruit-red dry class and 1st. Prize N.Y.S.D. Show 1976.

> 2 × 1 lb. (2 × 454 gm.) jars bilberries
> 15 oz. (425 gm.) tin black cherries
> 1 lb. (454 gm.) peeled over-ripe bananas
> 1¾ lb. (794 gm.) sugar as S.S.S.
> ⅛ teaspoon Epsom salts
> Pectin destroying enzyme
> 1 Campden tablet or 5 ml. strong sulphite solution
> 1 teaspoon malic acid
> 3 mg. vitamin B tablet
> All purpose or Bordeaux yeast starter
> Yeast nutrient
> Water to make up the volume to 7 pints (4 litres)

Method

Use Method 1, Chapter VI.

Strain the juice from the bilberries and cherries and measure the volume. Put the bilberries in a sterilised bucket; stone the cherries and add to the bilberries—crush the fruit. Add the fruit juices and the prepared banana 'gravy'. Pour over 2 pints (1.14 litres) of boiling water, cover cool, then add sulphite and pectin destroying enzyme. Leave covered 24 hours, then add all other ingredients, mix well, take an S.G. reading and subtract from 1.097 or 1.114. Ferment as usual, making S.S.S. additions as necessary, finishing with an S.G. of 0.990–1.000.

This wine is best drunk at six to nine months of age.

BILBERRY (2)
Wine style—Dry red table wine

> 2 × 1 lb. (2 × 454 gm.) jars bilberries
> 15 oz. (425 gm.) tin black cherries
> ¼ pint (142 ml.) red grape concentrate
> ½ lb. (227 gm.) peeled over-ripe bananas
> 1½ lb. (680 gm.) sugar as S.S.S.
> ½ cup of tea or 1/30 oz. (1 gm.) grape tannin
> Pectin destroying enzyme
> 3 mg. vitamin B tablet
> 1 Campden tablet or 5ml. strong sulphite solution
> All purpose or Bordeaux yeast starter
> Yeast nutrient
> Water to make up the volume to 7 pints (4 litres)

Method

Use Method 1, Chapter VI.

Prepare must as in Bilberry (1) adding the grape concentrate to the ingredients in the bucket, mix well, take an S.G. reading and subtract from 1.097 or 1.114. Ferment as usual, making S.S.S. additions where necessary, finishing with an S.G. of 0.990–1.000. Drink at about six to nine months.

BILBERRY (3)
Wine style—Dry red table wine
V.H.C.—Red dry table wine class—N.Y. & S.D. Show—1977

2 × 1 lb. (2 × 454 gm.) jars bilberries
15 oz. (425 gm.) tin blackcurrants
1 lb. (454 gm.) peeled over-ripe bananas
½ pint (284 ml.) red grape concentrate
1¼ lb. (567 gm.) sugar as S.S.S.
½ cup of tea or 1/30 oz. (1 gm.) grape tannin
Pectin destroying enzyme
3 mg. vitamin B tablet
All purpose or Burgundy yeast starter
Yeast nutrient
Water to make up the volume to 7 pints (4 litres)

Method

Use Method 1, Chapter VI.

Prepare as in previous recipe, mix well, take an S.G. reading and subtract from 1.097 or 1.114. Ferment as usual, finishing with an S.G. of 0.990–1.000. This being a slightly more full-bodied wine will keep somewhat longer than the two previous wines but is best drunk at about one year·

BILBERRY (4)
Wine style—Red dry table wine

2 × 1 lb. (2 × 454 gm.) jars bilberries
1 lb. (454 gm.) peeled over-ripe bananas
6 oz. (170 gm.) fresh elderberries
½ lb. (227 gm.) dried morello cherries
6 oz. (170 gm.) currants
1¼ lb. (567 gm.) sugar as S.S.S.
3 mg. vitamin B tablet
Pectin destroying enzyme
⅛ oz. (4 gm.) citric acid or acid mixture
All purpose or Burgundy yeast starter
Yeast nutrient
Water to make up the volume to 7 pints (4 litres)

Method

Pour ½ pint (284 ml.) boiling water over the cherries and soak over-night. Prepare the bilberries and bananas as in Bilberry (1); add the minced currants and crushed elderberries. Break up the cherries, removing the stones if convenient, and add to the other fruit. Pour over 2 pints (1.14 litres) of boiling water, cover, cool, then add sulphite and pectin destroying enzyme. Leave covered 24 hours then add all other ingredients, mix well, take an S.G. reading and subtract from 1.097 or 1.114. Ferment as usual, making S.S.S. additions as necessary, finishing with an S.G. of 0.990–1.000.

BILBERRY (5)
Wine style—Red dry table wine

2 × 1 lb. (2 × 454 gm.) jars bilberries
½ lb. (227 gm.) dried morello cherries
½ lb. (227 gm.) raisins
¾ lb. (340 gm.) peeled over-ripe bananas
1¼ lb. (567 gm.) sugar as S.S.S.
Pectin destroying enzyme
3 mg. vitamin B tablet
⅛ oz. (4 gm.) citric acid or acid mixture
1 Campden tablet or 5 ml. strong sulphite solution
All purpose or Burgundy yeast starter
Water to make up the volume to 7 pints (4 litres)

Method

Use Method 1, Chapter VI.

Prepare the must as in Bilberry (4), mix well, take an S.G. reading and subtract from 1.097 or 1.114. Ferment as usual, making S.S.S. additions as necessary, finishing with an S.G. of 0.990–1.000. This is a fairly full-bodied wine which will keep well.

BLACKBERRY (1)
Wine style—Dry red table wine

3 lb. (1.36 kilos) blackberries
½ lb. (227 gm.) sultanas
1¾ lb. (794 gm.) sugar as S.S.S.
Pectin destroying enzyme
3 mg. vitamin B tablet
1 Campden tablet or 5 ml. strong sulphite solution
All purpose or Bordeaux yeast starter
Yeast nutrient
Water to make up the volume to 7 pints (4 litres)

Method

Use Method 1, Chapter VI.

Crush the blackberries in a sterilised bucket and add the minced or liquidised sultanas. Pour over $2\frac{1}{2}$ pints (1.42 litres) boiling water, cover, cool and add sulphite and pectin destroying enzyme. Leave covered 24 hours, then add all other ingredients, mix well, take an S.G. reading and subtract from 1.097–1.114. Ferment as usual, making S.S.S. additions as necessary, finishing with an S.G. of 0.990–1.000.

BLACKBERRY (2)
Wine style—Dry red table wine

3 lb. (1.36 kilos) blackberries
1 lb. (454 gm.) peeled over-ripe bananas, plus two skins
$1\frac{3}{4}$ lb. (794 gm.) sugar as S.S.S.
Pectin destroying enzyme
3 mg. vitamin B tablet
1 Campden tablet or 5 ml. strong sulphite solution
All purpose or Bordeaux yeast starter
Water to make up the volume to 7 pints (4 litres)

Method

Use Method 1, Chapter VI.

Prepare blackberries as in Blackberry (1), and add prepared banana 'gravy'. Pour over $2\frac{1}{2}$ pints (1.42 litres) boiling water, cover, cool, and add sulphite and pectin destroying enzyme. Leave covered for 24 hours, then proceed as for Blackberry (1) finishing with an S.G. of 0.990–1.000.

BLACKBERRY (3)
Wine style—Red medium social wine

3 lb. (1.36 kilos) blackberries
$\frac{1}{2}$ lb (227 gm.) raisins
1 lb. (454 gm.) peeled over-ripe bananas
2 lb. (0.9 kilo) sugar as S.S.S.
3 mg. vitamin B tablet
Pectin destroying enzyme
1 Campden tablet or 5 ml. strong sulphite solution
All purpose yeast starter
Yeast nutrient
Water to make the volume up to 7 pints (4 litres)

Method

Use Method 1, Chapter VI.

Prepare the blackberries and dried fruit as in Blackberry (1), add the prepared banana 'gravy', and pour over $2\frac{1}{2}$ pints

(1.42 litres) boiling water, cool and add sulphite and pectin destroying enzyme. Leave covered 24 hours, then proceed as in previous recipe. Take an S.G. reading and subtract from 1.131. Ferment as usual, making S.S.S. additions as necessary, finishing with an S.G. of 1.006–1.014.

BLACKBERRY (4)
Wine style—Dry red table wine

2½ lb. (1.13 kilos) blackberries
¾ pint (426 ml.) red grape concentrate
1½ lb. (680 gm.) peeled over-ripe bananas
1¼ lb. (567 gm.) sugar as S.S.S.
3 mg. vitamin B tablet
Pectin destroying enzyme
1 Campden tablet or 5ml. strong sulphite solution
All purpose or Bordeaux yeast starter
Yeast nutrient
Water to make up the volume to 7 pints (4 litres)

Method

Use Method 1, Chapter VI.

Prepare blackberries and bananas as in Blackberry (2), add grape concentrate and 2½ pints (1.42 litres) boiling water. Cool and add sulphite and pectin destroying enzyme, leave covered 24 hours, then proceed as in Blackberry (1). Take an S.G. reading and subtract from 1.097 or 1.114. Ferment as usual, making S.S.S. additions as necessary, finishing with an S.G. of 0.990–1.000.

BLACKBERRY (5)
Wine style—Dry red table wine

By courtesy of Mr. D. G. Turner—Wine of the Year—Tyne-mouth Winemaking Society 1976 and frequent prizewinner in its class.

2 lb. (0.9 kilo) blackberries
½ lb. (227 gm.) elderberries
¼ can red grape concentrate
2 lb. (0.9 kilo) sugar
1 teaspoon tartaric or citric acid
Pectin destroying enzyme
All purpose or Bordeaux yeast starter
Yeast nutrient
1 Campden tablet

148

Method (*The method described below is Mr. Turner's own*)

Pick over the berries and wash under the tap. Pour over 2 pints (1.14 litres) boiling water. Cool and add one Campden tablet and pectin destroying enzyme. After 24 hours add 1 lb. (454 gm.) sugar, nutrient, acid, grape concentrate and yeast starter, with water to 5 pints (2.84 litres). After four days, strain through a nylon bag, add 8 oz. (227 gm.) sugar as syrup and make up to 7 pints (4 litres). After three-four days add the remaining sugar as syrup and top up with water. Ferment until dry—0.990–0.995. Allow to stand in a cold place for one to two days, and rack into a clean jar. Add one crushed Campden tablet and top up to the neck with water, or better with a dry wine. Store in a cool, dark place with fermentation lock initially and then with a bung. Rack again when crystal clear and allow to mature for at least six, preferably 12 months.

Alcohol content 13 % by volume. Acidity 3.5 p.p.t.

BLACKCURRANT (1)

Wine style—Dry red table wine

3 lb. (1.36 kilos) blackcurrants
1 lb. (454 gm.) peeled over-ripe bananas
1¾ lb. (794 gm.) sugar as S.S.S.
3 mg. vitamin B tablet
1 Campden tablet or 5 ml. strong sulphite solution
½ cup of tea or 1/30 oz. (1 gm.) grape tannin
Pectin destroying enzyme
All purpose or Bordeaux yeast starter
Yeast nutrient
Water to make up the volume to 7 pints (4 litres)

Method

Use Method 1, Chapter VI.

Crush the berries in a sterile bucket. Prepare and add banana 'gravy' and pour over 2½ pints (1.42 litres) boiling water. Cover, cool and add sulphite and pectin destroying enzyme. Leave 24 hours then add all other ingredients, mix well, take an S.G. reading and subtract from 1.097 or 1.114. Ferment as usual to an S.G. of 0.990–1.000 after S.S.S. additions.

BLACKCURRANT (2)
Wine style—Sweet red social wine
18 fl. oz. (511 ml.) bottle of blackcurrant syrup
¼ lb. (113 gm.) raisins
¼ lb. (113 gm.) sultanas
½ pint (284 ml.) red grape concentrate
1 lb. (454 gm.) peeled over-ripe bananas
1 lb. (454 gm.) sugar as S.S.S.
2, 3 mg. vitamin B tablets
Pectin destroying enzyme
All purpose yeast starter
Water to make up the volume to 7 pints (4 litres)

Method

Use Method 1, Chapter VI.

Bring the blackcurrant syrup to the boil and simmer for
three minutes, to remove excess preservative. Cool and pour
into a sterile bucket. Add minced or liquidised dried fruit,
grape concentrate, prepared banana 'gravy' and 1 pint
(568 ml.) boiling water. Cool and add sulphite and pectin
destroying enzyme. Leave covered for 24 hours then add all
other ingredients, mix well, take an S.G. reading and
subtract from 1.148. Ferment as usual, making S.S.S. additions
as necessary, finishing with an S.G. of 1.020.

BROOM (1) (or Gorse)
Wine style—White dry wine
4 pints (2.27 litres) Broom flowers
½ pint (284 ml.) white grape concentrate
1½ lb. (680 gm.) sugar as S.S.S.
2 oranges
1 lemon
1 Campden tablet or 5 ml. strong sulphite solution
2, 3 mg. vitamin B tablets
½ cup of tea or 1/30 oz. (1 gm.) grape tannin
Pectin destroying enzyme
All purpose or Burgundy yeast starter
Yeast nutrient
Yeast energiser
Water to make up the volume to 7 pints (4 litres)

Method

Use Method 1, Chapter VI.

Put the flowers into a sterilised bucket and pour over
3 pints (1.7 litres) boiling water. Add the juice and finely
grated peel and juice of the oranges and lemon. Cover and
when cool, add sulphite and pectin destroying enzyme and

leave 24 hours. Next day add all other ingredients, mix well, take an S.G. reading and subtract from 1.097 or 1.114. Ferment as usual, making S.S.S. additions as necessary finishing with an S.G. of 0.990–1.000.

BROOM (2) (or Gorse)
Wine style—Medium social wine
4 pints (2.27 litres) Broom flowers
6 oz. (170 gm.) sultanas
2 lb. (0.9 kilo) sugar as S.S.S.
2 oranges
1 lemon
½ cup of tea or 1/30 oz. (1 gm.) grape tannin
1 Campden tablet or 5 ml. strong sulphite solution
2, 3 mg. vitamin B tablets
Pectin destroying enzyme
All purpose yeast starter
Yeast nutrient
Yeast energiser
Water to make up the volume to 7 pints (4 litres)

Method

Use Method 1, Chapter VI.

Put flowers and minced or liquidised sultanas in a sterilised bucket. Finely grate the peel of the oranges and lemon, boil in a little water for five minutes, strain and add the liquor to the bucket. Pour over 3 pints (1.7 litres) boiling water, cover, cool and add sulphite and pectin destroying enzyme. Leave 24 hours then add all other ingredients including the juice of the citrus fruits. Mix well, take an S.G. reading and subtract from 1.131. Ferment as usual, making S.S.S. additions as necessary, finishing with an S.G. of 1.006–1.014.

BROOM (3) (or Gorse)
Wine style—Sweet white social wine
4 pints (2.27 litres) Broom flowers
¾ lb. (340 gm.) raisins
2 lb. (0.9 kilo) sugar as S.S.S.
2 oranges
1 lemon
2, 3 mg. vitamin B tablets
1 Campden tablet or 5 ml. strong sulphite solution
Pectin destroying enzyme
½ cup of tea or 1/30 oz. (1 gm.) grape tannin
All purpose or Sauternes yeast starter
Yeast nutrient
Water to make up the volume to 7 pints (4 litres)

Method

Use Method 1, Chapter VI.

Follow the procedures for Broom (2), subtracting the S.G. from 1.148. The final S.G. should be 1.020.

BURNET (1)

Wine style—Dry red table wine

3rd. Prize—Dry flower wine class—Yorkshire Federation Show, 1973

A sweeter, higher alcohol version of the same wine won 2nd. Prize in the Sweet flower wine class in the same show.

> 5 pints (2.84 litres) Burnet flowers
> ¼ lb. (113 gm.) sultanas
> 1¾ lb. (794 gm.) sugar as S.S.S.
> Juice 1 lemon
> ¼ oz. (7 gm.) tartaric acid
> 2, 3 mg. vitamin B tablets
> All purpose or Burgundy yeast starter
> Yeast nutrient
> Yeast energiser
> 1 Campden tablet or 5 ml. strong sulphite solution
> Water to make up the volume to 7 pints (4 litres)

Method

Use Method 1, Chapter VI.

Put the flowers and minced or liquidised dried fruit into a sterilised bucket and pour over 3 pints (1.7 litres) of boiling water. Cover, cool and add sulphite and pectin destroying enzyme—leave covered 24 hours then add all other ingredients, mix well, take an S.G. reading and subtract from 1.097 or 1.114. Ferment as usual, making S.S.S. additions as necessary, finishing with an S.G. of 0.990–1.000.

This wine is a surprisingly good deep red colour and is fairly full-bodied considering that it is a flower wine. These qualities have caused some controversy in shows at times.

BURNET (2)

Wine style—Sweet red Port-like or social wine

1st. Prize—Sweet flower wine class—National Show 1972

        5 pints (2.84 litres) Burnet flowers
        ½ lb. (227 gm.) sultanas
        2¼ lb. (1.02 kilos) sugar as S.S.S.
        Juice 1 lemon
        ¼ oz. (7 gm.) tartaric acid
        ⅛ oz. (3.5 gm.) citric acid
        2, 3 mg. vitamin B tablets
        All purpose or Port yeast starter
        Yeast nutrient
        Yeast energiser
        1 Campden tablet or 5 ml. strong sulphite solution
        Water to make up the volume to 7 pints (4 litres)

Method

Use Method 1, Chapter VI.

Prepare as in previous recipe and subtract the S.G. from 1.148. Ferment as usual, finishing with an S.G. of 1.020 after S.S.S. additions.

This wine, like the previous one, has also caused controversy in shows because of its rich, full bodied character.

BURNET (3)

Wine style—Sweet social wine (Port-like)

        5 pints (2.84 litres) Burnet flowers
        ½ lb. (227 gm.) currants or raisins
        ½ pint (284 ml.) red grape concentrate
        1¾ lb. (794 gm.) sugar as S.S.S.
        Pectin destroying enzyme
        1 lemon
        ½ cup tea or 1/30 oz. (1 gm.) grape tannin
        1 Campden tablet or 5 ml. strong sulphite solution
        All purpose or Port yeast starter
        Yeast nutrient
        Yeast energiser
        Water to make up the volume to 7 pints (4 litres)

Method

Use Method 1, Chapter VI.

Prepare flowers and dried fruit as in Burnet (1) and add grape concentrate. Finely grate the peel of the lemon, pour over ¼ pint (142 ml.) boiling water and leave to infuse for 24 hours, then make up the must as usual, adding the strained infusion from the peel. Mix well, taken an S.G. reading and

153

subtract from 1.148. Ferment as usual making S.S.S. additions as necessary, finishing with an S.G. of 1.020.

N.B. All Burnet wines are at their best at about nine months to one year.

CLOVER (1)
Wine style—Dry white table wine
4 pints (2.27 litres) white clover flowers
½ lb. (227 gm.) sultanas
1¾ lb. (794 gm.) sugar as S.S.S.
1 lemon
2 oranges
½ cup tea or 1/30 oz. (1 gm.) grape tannin
2, 3 mg. vitamin B tablets
1 Campden tablet or 5 ml. strong sulphite solution
All purpose or Burgundy yeast starter
Yeast nutrient
Yeast energiser
Water to make up the volume to 7 pints (4 litres)

Method

Use Method 1, Chapter VI.

Place the flowers and minced dried fruit, lemon and orange juice, in a clean bucket and pour over 2½ pints (1.42 litres) boiling water. Cover, cool, add sulphite and pectin destroying enzyme and leave 24 hours. Then add all other ingredients, mix well, take S.G. reading and subtract from 1.097 or 1.114. Ferment as usual, making S.S.S. additions as necessary, finishing with an S.G. reading of 0.990–1.000.

CLOVER (2)
Wine style—Medium sweet social wine
6 pints (3.4 litres) clover flowers (pink or white)
¾ lb. (340 gm.) sultanas
2 lb. (0.9 kilo) sugar as S.S.S.
1 cup tea or 1/15 oz. (2 gm.) grape tannin
¼ oz. (7 gm.) citric aicd or ⅜ oz. (11 gm.) acid mixture
2, 3 mg. vitamin B tablets
All purpose yeast starter
Yeast nutrient
Yeast energiser
1 Campden tablet or 5 ml. strong sulphite solution
Water to make up the volume to 7 pints (4 litres)

Method

Use Method 1, Chapter VI.

Prepare in the same way as in Clover (1), subtract the S.G. from 1.131. Ferment as usual, making S.S.S. additions as necessary, finishing with an S.G. of 1.006–1.014.

CARROT
Wine style—Medium social wine
4 lb. (1.8 kilos) carrots
2¼ lb. (1.02 kilos) sugar as S.S.S.
⅝ oz. (18 gm.) citric acid or acid mixture
1 cup tea or 1/15 oz. (2 gm.) grape tannin
3 mg. vitamin B tablet
All purpose yeast starter
Yeast nutrient
Water to make up the volume to 7 pints (4 litres)

Method
Use Method 3, Chapter VI.

Scrub and dice the carrots and boil or pressure cook as described in Method 3, Chapter VI. Strain off the liquor and measure the volume—pour into a clean demijohn. Add all other ingredients, mix well, take an S.G. reading and subtract from 1.131. Ferment as usual, making S.S.S. additions as necessary, finishing with an S.G. of 1.006–1.014.

A fuller bodied wine may be prepared by including ½ lb. (227 gm.) minced or liquidised dried fruit in the recipe, in which case a pulp fermentation may be conducted using the carrot liquor and the dried fruit, Alternatively the dried fruit may be boiled or pressure cooked and the strained liquor added to the carrot juice in the demijohn with the other recipe ingredients. Ferment as usual.

CHERRY (1)
Wine style—Medium sweet social wine
1 lb. (454 gm.) dried Morello cherries
1 lb. (454 gm.) peeled over-ripe bananas
1¾ lb. (794 gm.) sugar as S.S.S.
½ oz. (14 gm.) acid mixture or ⅜ oz. (11 gm.) citric acid
3 mg. vitamin B tablet
All purpose yeast starter
Yeast nutrient
Water to make up the volume to 7 pints (4 litres)

Method
Use Method 3, Chapter VI.

Boil or pressure cook the dried cherries for ¾ hour or 15 minutes respectively, to reconstitute them. Prepare banana 'gravy'. Measure the volume of the strained cherry and banana liquors and when cool pour into a clean demijohn or ferment on the cherry pulp in a bucket if preferred. Prepare the must as usual, mix well, take an S.G. reading and subtract from 1.131. Ferment as usual, making S.S.S. additions as necessary, finishing with an S.G. of 1.010–1.014.

CHERRY (2)
By courtesy of Mr. B. Campbell—Tynemouth Winemaking Soc.

Wine style—Sweet red wine
2 lb. (0.9 kilo) jar Krakus Morello Cherries
6 oz. (170 gm.) dried bananas
1 teaspoon citric acid
1 teaspoon tannin
3 lb. (1.3 kilo) sugar
1 teaspoon Tronozymol nutrient
1 teaspoon pectin destroying enzyme
1 sachet dried all purpose yeast

Method

Chop the bananas finely and put into a pan with 2 pints (1.14 litres) hot water. When soft, bring to the boil and simmer for 20 minutes. Meanwhile, put the cherries and 2 lb. (0.9 kilo) sugar into a bucket and pour over 3 pints (1.7 litres) boiling water, stirring well, crushing the cherries. Empty the bananas and liquid into the bucket and add 1 pint (568 ml.) cold water, stir, cover and cool. Add pectin destroying enzyme, acid, tannin, nutrient and yeast—stir. Cover and ferment on the pulp for four days then strain into a demijohn, fitting an airlock. After seven days add the remaining sugar as S.S.S. and top up with cold water. Mix well. When fermentation ceases, rack and add 1 Campden tablet. Repeat this two months later and after another month the wine should be ready to bottle.

COLTSFOOT
Wine style—Medium social wine
6 pints (3.4 litres) Coltsfoot flowers
½ lb. (227 gm.) sultanas
2 lb. (0.9 kilo) sugar as S.S.S.
2 oranges
2 lemons
½ cup tea or 1/30 oz. (1 gm.) grape tannin
2, 3 mg. vitamin B tablets
1 Campden tablet or 5 ml. strong sulphite solution
All purpose yeast starter
Yeast nutrient
Yeast energiser
Water to make up the volume to 7 pints (4 litres)

Method

Use Method 1, Chapter VI.

Remove as much greenery as possible from the flowers and place them in a clean bucket with the minced or liquidised sultanas. Add the finely grated peel and the measured juice from the oranges and lemons and pour over 2½ pints (1.42 litres) boiling water. Cover, cool and add sulphite and pectin destroying enzyme. Leave covered for 24 hours then make up the must as usual, mix well, take an S.G. reading and subtract from 1.131. Ferment as usual, making S.S.S. additions as necessary finishing with an S.G. of 1.006–1.014.

CURRANT (1) (Dried Fruit)

Wine style—Medium social wine

1 lb. (454 gm.) currants
1¾ lb. (794 gm.) sugar as S.S.S.
3 mg. vitamin B tablet
Pectin destroying enzyme
All purpose yeast starter
Yeast nutrient
Water to make up the volume to 7 pints (4 litres)

Method

Use Method 3, Chapter VI.

Mince and boil or pressure cook the currants in 2–3 pints (1.14–1.7 litres) water for 1 hour or 15 minutes respectively. Strain and cool the liquor and pour into a clean demijohn. Add all other ingredients, mix well, taken an S.G. reading and subtract from 1.131. Ferment as usual, making S.S.S. additions as necessary finishing with an S.G. of 1.006–1.014.

CURRANT (2) (Dried fruit)

Wine style—Sweet social wine or Sherry type

2 lb. (09 kilo) currants
1½ lb. (6.80 gm.) sugar as S.S.S.
3 oranges
3 gm. vitamin B tablet
All purpose or Sherry yeast starter
Yeast nutrient
Pectin destroying enzyme
Water to make up the volume to 7 pints (4 litres)

Method

Use Method 3, Chapter VI.

Infuse the finely grated peel of the oranges in ½ pint (284 ml.) boiling water and leave 24 hours. Next day prepare the currants as in the previous recipe, strain and pour the cooled liquor into a clean demijohn. Add the strained liquor from the peel and squeezed oranges and all other ingredients. Mix well, take an S.G. reading and subtract from 1.148. Ferment as usual, making S.S.S. additions as necessary, finishing with an S.G. of 1.020. Do not sulphite at the first racking so that oxidation may occur. The vessel should be only 5/6 full and the neck plugged with cotton wool during maturation. The development of a true Sherry-like flavour may take many months in glass but may be considerably hastened by maturing in a thin polythene container. Once the Sherry character has been achieved, bottle and mature for another one to two years preferably.

DAMSON

Wine style—Dessert wine

8 lb. (3.63 kilos) fully ripe damsons
½ pint (284 ml.) red grape concentrate
2 lb. (0.9 kilo) peeled over-ripe bananas
1½ lb. (680 gm.) sugar as S.S.S.
3 mg. vitamin B tablet
Pectin destroying enzyme
All purpose or Port type yeast starter
Yeast nutrient
1 Campden tablet or 5 ml. strong sulphite solution
Water to make up the volume to 7 pints (4 litres)

Method

Use Method 1, Chapter VI.

Wash and stone the fruit and crush in a sterile bucket. Add prepared banana 'gravy' and 2 pints (1.14 litres) boiling water. Cover, cool and add sulphite and pectin destroying enzyme. Leave 24 hours, then add all other ingredients, mix well, take an S.G. reading and subtract from 1.148. Ferment as usual, making S.S.S. additions as necessary, finishing with an S.G. of 1.020. The acidity of this wine may have to be reduced in which case precipitated chalk or potassium carbonate may be utilised (see Chapter V, p. 72).

DANDELION

Wine style—Medium dry social wine

4 pints (2.27 litres) dandelion flowers
½ lb. (227 gm.) raisins
2 oranges
2 lb. (0.9 kilo) sugar as S.S.S.
1 Campden tablet or 5 ml. strong sulphite solution
⅜ oz. (11 gm.) acid mixture or ¼ oz. (7 gm.) citric acid
2, 3 mg. vitamin B tablets
Pectin destroying enzyme
½ cup tea or 1/30 oz. (1 gm.) grape tannin
All purpose or Bordeaux yeast
Yeast nutrient
Yeast energiser
Water to make up the volume to 4 pints (7 litres)

Method

Use Method 1, Chapter VI.

Remove all greenery from the flowers and place them in a clean bucket. Add minced or liquidised raisins and the finely grated peel of the oranges. Pour over 2 pints (1.14 litres) boiling water, cover, cool and then add sulphite and pectin destroying enzyme. Leave covered 24 hours then add the juice of the oranges and all other ingredients, mix well, take an S.G. reading and subtract from 1.114. Ferment as usual, making S.S.S. additions as necessary, finishing with an S.G. of 1.004–1.010.

DATE

Wine style—Sweet social or Sherry type

2 lb. (0.9 kilo) dates
4 lb. (1.8 kilos) mixed apples
½ pint (284 ml.) white grape concentrate
¾ lb (340 gm.) brown sugar as S.S.S.
3 mg. vitamin B tablet
1 Campden tablet or 5 ml. strong sulphite solution
All purpose or Sherry yeast
Yeast nutrient
Pectin destroying enzyme
Water to make up the volume to 7 pints (4 litres)

Method

Use Method 1, Chapter VI.

Chop the apples and add to 2 pints (1.14 litres) cold water containing sulphite in a clean bucket. Mince or liquidise the dates and boil or pressure cook for 1 hour or 15 minutes respectively, in 2 pints (1.14 litres) water. Strain off the liquor, cool, measure the volume and add to the apples in the bucket. Add pectin destroying enzyme, and leave covered 24 hours, then add all other ingredients, mix well, take an S.G. reading and subtract from 1.148. Ferment as usual, making S.S.S. additions as necessary, finishing with an S.G. of 1.020. Rack and mature as described in Currant (2) to produce a true Sherry-like flavour.

ELDERFLOWER (1)

Wine style—Dry white table wine

¾ pint (426 ml.) elderflowers
½ lb. (227 gm.) sultanas or raisins
1¾ lb. (794 gm.) sugar as S.S.S.
1½ lemons
2, 3 mg. vitamin B tablets
1 Campden tablet or 5 ml. strong sulphite solution
Pectin destroying enzyme
All purpose or Bordeaux yeast starter
Pectin destroying enzyme
½ cup tea or 1/30 oz. (1 gm.) grape tannin
Yeast nutrient
Yeast energiser
Water to make up the volume to 7 pints (4 litres)

Method

Use Method 1, Chapter VI.

Cut the flowers off the stems and place them in a clean bucket. Mince or liquidise the dried fruit, finely grate the peel of the lemons and squeeze out the juice and add to the bucket. Pour over 2 pints (1.14 litres) boiling water, cool and add sulphite and pectin destroying enzyme. Leave covered 24 hours then add all other ingredients, mix well, take an S.G. reading and subtract from 1.097 or 1.114. Ferment as usual, making S.S.S. additions as necessary, finishing with an S.G. of 0.990–1.000.

ELDERFLOWER (2)
Wine style—Dry white table wine
¾ pint (426 ml.) elderflowers
½ pint (284 ml.) white grape concentrate
1½ lb. (680 gm.) sugar as S.S.S.
½ cup tea or 1/30 oz. (1 gm.) grape tannin
⅜ oz. (11 gm.) mixed acids or ¼ oz. (7 gm.) citric acid
Pectin destroying enzyme
2, 3 mg. vitamin B tablets
1 Campden tablet or 5 ml. strong sulphite solution
All purpose or Bordeaux yeast
Yeast nutrient
Yeast energiser
Water to make up the volume to 7 pints (4 litres)

Method

Use Method 1, Chapter VI.

Prepare flowers as in elderflower (1), add grape concentrate and pour over 2 pints (1.14 litres) boiling water, cover, cool and add sulphite and pectin destroying enzyme. Leave covered 24 hours then add all other ingredients, mix well, take an S.G. reading and subtract from 0.097 or 1.114. Ferment as usual, making S.S.S. additions as necessary, finishing with an S.G. of 0.990–1.000.

ELDERFLOWER (3)
Wine style—Medium table wine
This wine is very much like a Liebfraumilch.
¾ pint (426 ml.) elderflowers
¼ lb. (113 gm.) muscatel raisins
¼ lb. (113 gm.) sultanas
2 lb. (0.9 kilo) sugar as S.S.S.
⅜ oz. (11 gm.) acid mixture or ¼ oz. (7 gm.) citric acid
2, 3 mg. vitamin B tablets
1 Campden tablet or 5 ml. strong sulphite solution
Pectin destroying enzyme
All purpose or Liebfraumilch yeast
Yeast nutrient
Yeast energiser
Water to make up the volume to 7 pints (4 litres)

Method

Use Method 1, Chapter VI.

Prepare flowers as in previous recipes. Add minced or liquidised muscatel raisins and sultanas and pour over

161

2 pints (1.14 litres) boiling water. Cover, cool and add sulphite and pectin destroying enzyme. Leave covered 24 hours then add all other ingredients, mix well, take an S.G. reading and subtract from 1.114. Ferment as usual, making S.S.S. additions as necessary, finishing with an S.G. of 1.006–1.010.

This wine can be made into a sweet wine by increasing the alcohol content during fermentation and finishing with an SG of 1.020.

ELDERFLOWER (4)

Wine style—Sweet social wine

¾ pint (426 ml.) elderflowers
½ pint (284 ml.) white grape concentrate
2 lb. (0.9 kilo) sugar as S.S.S.
1½ lb. (680 gm.) peeled over-ripe bananas (plus ½ skins)
½ oz. (14 gm.) mixed acids or ⅜ oz. (11 gm.) citric acid
2, 3 mg. vitamin tablets
1 Campden tablet or 5 ml. strong sulphite solution
Pectin destroying enzyme
All purpose or Sauternes yeast starter
Yeast nutrient
Yeast energiser
Water to make up the volume to 7 pints (4 litres)

Method

Use Method 1, Chapter VI.

Prepare flowers as in previous recipes and add the grape concentrate, prepared banana 'gravy' and 2 pints (1.14 litres) boiling water. Cover, cool and add sulphite and pectin destroying enzyme. Leave covered 24 hours then add all other ingredients, mix well, take an S.G. reading and subtract from 1.020.

ELDERBERRY

In a poor season, the tannin content of elderberries may be very high so that no tannin need be added to the wine, but in a normal to very good season, some tannin should be included to ensure that the wine will have the necessary astringency. Commonsense must be employed with regard to this matter. The following recipes are formulated on the assumption that the berries have fully ripened during a good season.

ELDERBERRY (1)
Wine style—Dry red table wine

3 lb. (1.36 kilos) elderberries
2 lb. (0.9 kilo) sugar as S.S.S.
1 cup tea or 1/15 oz. (2 gm.) grape tannin
3 mg. vitamin B tablet
¼ oz. (7 gm.) mixed acids or citric acid
1 Campden tablet or 5 ml. strong sulphite solution
Pectin destroying enzyme
All purpose or Bordeaux yeast starter
Yeast nutrient
Water to make up the volume to 7 pints (4 litres)

Method

Use Method 1, Chapter VI.

Strig the elderberries from the stems with a fork. Put in a sterile bucket, crush and add 2½ pints (1.42 litres) boiling water. Cover, cool and add sulphite and pectin destroying enzyme. Leave covered 24 hours then add all other ingredients, mix well, take S.G. reading and subtract from 1.097 or 1.114. Ferment as usual, making S.S.S. additions as necessary, finishing with an S.G. of 0.990–1.000.

ELDERBERRY (2)
Wine style—Dry red table wine

2½ lb. (1.13 kilos) elderberries
2 lb. (0.9 kilo) mixed apples
1¾ lb. (794 gm.) sugar as S.S.S.
½ cup tea or 1/30 oz. (1 gm.) grape tannin
3 mg. vitamin B tablet
Pectin destroying enzyme
1 Campden tablet or 5 ml. strong sulphite solution
All purpose or Burgundy yeast starter
Yeast nutrient
Water to make up the volume to 7 pints (4 litres)

Method

Use Method 1, Chapter VI.

Prepare elderberries as in previous recipes. Pour over 2½ pints (1.42 litres) boiling water, cover, cool and add sulphite and pectin destroying enzyme. Wash and chop up apples into small chunks and add to the elderberries. Leave covered 24 hours then add all other ingredients, mix well, take an S.G. reading and subtract from 1.097 or 1.114. Ferment as usual, making S.S.S. additions as necessary, finishing with an S.G. of 0.990–1.000.

ELDERBERRY (3)
Wine style—Dry red table wine
Medium dry version won 3rd prize—N.W. Federation Show
1976

3 lb. (1.36 kilos) elderberries
1 lb. (454 gm.) peeled over-ripe bananas
1¾ lb. (794 gm.) sugar as S.S.S.
1 cup tea or 1/15 oz. (2 gm.) grape tannin
3 mg. vitamin B tablet
1 Campden tablet or 5 ml. strong sulphite solution
¼ oz. (7 gm.) mixed acids or citric acid
Pectin destroying enzyme
All purpose or Burgundy yeast starter
Yeast nutrient
Water to make up the volume to 7 pints (4 litres)

Method

Use Method 1, Chapter VI.

Prepare elderberries as in previous recipes. Add prepared banana 'gravy' and 2 pints (1.14 litres) boiling water. Cover, cool and add sulphite and pectin destroying enzyme. Leave covered 24 hours then add all other ingredients, mix well and take an S.G. reading—subtract from 1.097–1.114. Ferment as usual making S.S.S. additions as necessary, finishing with an S.G. of 0.990–1.000.

ELDERBERRY (4)
Wine style—Dry red table wine

2½ lb. (1.13 kilos) elderberries
½ lb. (227 gm.) sultanas
1 lb. (454 gm.) peeled over-ripe bananas
½ oz. (14 gm.) dried or 1 pint (568 ml.) fresh scented rose petals
1¾ lb. (794 gm.) sugar as S.S.S.
3 mg. vitamin B tablet
¼ cup tea or 1/30 oz. (1 gm.) grape tannin
1 Campden tablet or 5 ml. strong sulphite solution
Pectin destroying enzyme
All purpose or Rhone yeast starter
Yeast nutrient
Water to make up the volume to 7 pints (4 litres)

Method

Use Method 1, Chapter VI.

Prepare elderberries as in Elderberry (1) and add minced or liquidised sultanas, prepared banana 'gravy' and rose petals. Pour over 2 pints (1.14 litres) boiling water. Cover, cool and add sulphite and pectin destroying enzyme. Leave covered

24 hours then add all other ingredients, mix well, take an S.G. reading and subtract from 1.097 or 1.114. Ferment as usual, making S.S.S. additions as necessary, finishing with an S.G. of 0.990–1.000.

ELDERBERRY (5)
Wine style—Sweet social wine
3rd Prize—Sweet elderberry wine class—National 1975

3 lb. (1.36 kilos) elderberries
½ lb. (227 gm.) raisins
2¼ lb. (1.02 kilos) sugar as S.S.S.
1 cup tea or 1/15 oz. (2 gm.) grape tannin
3 mg. vitamin B tablet
1 Campden tablet or 5 ml. strong sulphite solution
¼ oz. (7 gm.) mixed acids or citric acid
All purpose or Burgundy yeast starter
Pectin destroying enzyme
Yeast nutrient
Water to make up the volume to 7 pints (4 litres)

Method

Use Method 1, Chapter VI.

Prepare elderberries as in previous recipes and add minced or liquidised raisins, and 2 pints (1.14 litres) boiling water. Cover, cool and add sulphite and pectin destroying enzyme. Leave covered for 24 hours then add all other ingredients, mix well, take an S.G. reading and subtract from 1.148. Ferment as usual, making S.S.S. additions as necessary, finishing with an S.G. of 1.020

ELDERBERRY (6)
Wine style—Medium sweet social wine

1½ lb.) (680 gm.) elderberries
1½ lb. (680 gm.) blackberries
½ pint (284 ml.) red grape concentrate
1 lb. (454 gm.) peeled over-ripe bananas
3 mg. vitamin B tablet
1 Campden tablet or 5 ml. strong sulphite solution
Pectin destroying enzyme
1½ lb. (680 gm.) sugar as S.S.S.
All purpose or Burgundy yeast starter
Yeast nutrient
Water to make up the volume to 7 pints (4 litres)

Method

Use Method, 1, Chapter VI.

Crush the elderberries and blackberries in a sterile bucket

and add the grape concentrate and prepared banana 'gravy'. Pour over 2 pints (1.14 litres) boiling water, cool and add sulphite and pectin destroying enzyme. Leave covered 24 hours then add all other ingredients, mix well, take an S.G. reading and subtract from 1.131. Ferment as usual, making S.S.S. additions as necessary, finishing with an S.G. of 1.006–1.014.

ELDERBERRY (7)
Wine style—Dry red table wine
2½ lb. (1.13 kilos) elderberries
¾ lb. (340 gm.) rosehips
2 lb. (0.9 kilo) sugar as S.S.S.
¼ oz. (7 gm.) mixed acids or ⅛ oz. (4 gm.) citric acid
Juice 2 oranges
½ cup tea or 1/30 oz. (1 gm.) grape tannin
3 mg. vitamin B tablet
Pectin destroying enzyme
1 Campden tablet or 5 ml. strong sulphite solution
All purpose or Burgundy yeast starter
Yeast nutrient
Water to make up the volume to 7 pints (4 litres)

Method

Use Method 1, Chapter VI.

Crush the elderberries in a sterilised bucket, add minced rosehips and pour over 2 pints (1.14 litres) boiling water. Cover, cool and add sulphite and pectin destroying enzyme. Leave covered 24 hours then add all other ingredients, mix well, take an S.G. reading and subtract from 1.097 or 1.114. Ferment as usual, making S.S.S. additions as necessary, finishing with an S.G. of 0.990–1.000.

ELDERBERRY (8)
Wine style—Dessert red wine
3½ lb. (1.59 kilos) elderberries
½ lb. (227 gm.) raisins
2 lb. (0.9 kilo) peeled over-ripe bananas
½ pint (284 ml.) cherry and black grape concentrate
1½ lb. (680 gm.) sugar as S.S.S.
3 mg. vitamin B tablet
⅜ oz. (11 gm.) acid mixture or ¼ oz. (7 gm.) citric acid
1 Campden tablet or 5 ml. strong sulphite solution
1 cup tea or 1/15 oz. (2 gm.) grape tannin
Pectin destroying enzyme
All purpose or Port yeast starter
Yeast nutrient
Water to make up the volume to 7 pints (4 litres)

Method

Use Method 1, Chapter VI

Crush the elderberries in a bucket and add minced or liquidised raisins, cherry and black grape concentrate and prepared banana 'gravy'. Pour over 2 pints (1.14 litres) boiling water, cover, cool and add sulphite and pectin destroying enzyme. Leave covered 24 hours then add all other ingredients, mix well, take an S.G. reading and subtract from 1.148. Ferment as usual, making S.S.S. additions as necessary, finishing with an S.G. of 1.020.

ELDERBERRY (9)

Wine style—Dessert red wine

H.C. Sweet red social wine class—N.Y. & S.D. Show 1977

4 lb. (1.8 kilos) elderberries
¾ pint (426 ml.) grape and morello cherry concentrate
2 lb. (0.9 kilo) peeled over-ripe bananas plus 4 skins
½ lb. (227 gm.) muscatel raisins
1¼ lb. (567 gm.) sugar as S.S.S.
3 mg. vitamin B tablet
Pectin destroying enzyme
1 Campden tablet or 5 ml. strong sulphite solution
1 cup tea or 1/15 oz. (2 gm.) grape tannin
All purpose or Port yeast starter
Yeast nutrient
Water to make up the volume to 7 pints (4 litres)

Method Use Method 1, Chapter VI.

Prepare the must as in Elderberry (8). Ferment as usual, making S.S.S. additions as necessary, finishing with an S.G. of 1.020.

ELDERBERRY (10)

Wine style—Dessert red wine

3 lb. (1.36 kilos) elderberries
1 lb. (454 gm.) blackberries
2 lb. (0.9 kilos) peeled over-ripe bananas
½ lb. (227 gm.) raisins
2 lb. (0.9 kilo) sugar as S.S.S.
3 mg. vitamin B tablet
Yeast nutrient
Pectin destroying enzyme
1 cup tea or 1/15 oz. (2 gm.) grape tannin
1 Campden tablet or 5 ml. strong sulphite solution
All purpose or Port yeast starter
Water to make up the volume to 7 pints (4 litres)

Method

Use Method 1, Chapter VI.

Prepare the must as in Elderberry (8) adding the blackberries to the elderberries in the bucket. Ferment as usual, making S.S.S. additions as necessary, finishing with an S.G. of 1.020.

ELDERBERRY (11)

Wine style—Dry red table wine

By courtesy of Mr. B. Campbell—Tynemouth Winemaking Society

8 oz. (227 gm.) dried elderberries

8 oz. (227 gm.) dried rosehips

6 oz. (170 gm.) dried bananas

1 teaspoon citric acid

1 teaspoon Tronozymol nutrient

1 teaspoon pectin destroying enzyme

1 sachet all purpose yeast

2 lb. (0.9 kilo) sugar

Method

Put the elderberries and rosehips into a pan with 3 pints (1.7 litres) boiling water. Allow to stand until soft then simmer for five minutes. Chop the bananas finely, put into a pan with 2 pints (1.14 litres) hot water and when soft bring to the boil and simmer for 20 minutes. Put the sugar into a bucket and when ready, pour in the elderberries, rosehips, bananas and liquid. Stir well and make up to approximately 7 pints (4 litres) with cold water. When cool add other ingredients, again stirring well. Cover and ferment on the pulp for four days, Strain into a demijohn and when ferment quietens, top up to the neck with cold water. When fermentation ceases, rack and add 1 soluble Campden tablet. Repeat after two months and after another two months the wine is ready to bottle.

1st Prize—dry red wine class—Tynemouth Winemaking Society—Annual competition—1977.

FENNEL
Wine style—Medium social wine
5 pints (2.84 litres) fennel leaves
½ lb. (227 gm.) sultanas
2 lb. (0.9 kilo) sugar as S.S.S.
2, 3 mg. vitamin B tablets
1 cup tea or 1/15 oz. (2 gm.) grape tannin
⅜ oz. (11 gm.) acid mixture or ¼ oz. (7 gm.) citric acid
Pectin destroying enzyme
1 Campden tablet or 5 ml. strong sulphite solution
All purpose yeast starter
Yeast nutrient
Yeast energiser
Water to make up the volume to 7 pints (4 litres)

Method

Use Method 1, Chapter VI.

Pour 2½ pints (1.42 litres) boiling water over the fennel leaves in a clean bucket and add the minced or liquidised sultanas. Cover, cool and add sulphite and pectin destroying enzyme. Leave covered 24 hours then add all other ingredients, mix well, take an S.G. reading and subtract from 1.131. Ferment as usual, making S.S.S. additions as necessary, finishing with an S.G. of 1.006–1.014.

FIG
Wine style—Medium sweet social wine
½ lb. (227 gm.) figs
1 bottle Quosh Tropical fruit cordial
1½ lb. (680 gm.) sugar as S.S.S.
1 cup tea or 1/15 oz. (2 gm.) grape tannin
2, 3 mg. vitamin B tablets
All purpose yeast starter
Yeast nutrient
Yeast energiser
Water to make up the volume to 7 pints (4 litres)

Method

Use Method 1, Chapter VI.

Mince or liquidise the figs and pour over 2 pints (1.14 litres) boiling water in a sterilised bucket. Simmer the cordial for three minutes to remove excess preservative then add to the bucket. Cover, cool and add sulphite and pectin destroying enzyme. Leave covered 24 hours then add all other ingredients, mix well, take an S.G. reading and subtract from 1.131. Ferment as usual making S.S.S. additions as necessary, finishing with an S.G. of 1.006–1.014.

GOOSEBERRY (1)
Wine style—Dry white table wine (Hock type)

Tinned gooseberries are used in most of the following gooseberry recipes and since they are usually skinned, tannin should be added to the must.

> 3×1 lb. 3 oz. (540 gm.) tins gooseberries
> (equivalent to 2lb. fresh gooseberries)
> 1 lb. (454 gm.) peeled over-ripe bananas
> $\frac{1}{2}$ pint (284 ml.) white grape concentrate
> $\frac{1}{2}$ cup tea or 1/30 oz. (1 gm.) grape tannin
> $1\frac{1}{4}$ lb. (567 gm.) sugar as S.S.S.
> 3 mg. vitamin B tablet
> All purpose or Hock yeast starter
> Yeast nutrient
> Pectin destroying enzyme
> Water to make up the volume to 7 pints (4 litres)

Method

Use Method 1, Chapter VI.

Drain the gooseberries and crush in a sterilised bucket. Measure the amount of gooseberry syrup and add to the bucket. Pour over 2 pints (1.14 litres) boiling water and add prepared banana 'gravy' and grape concentrate. Cover, cool and add sulphite and pectin destroying enzyme. Leave covered 24 hours then add all other ingredients, mix well, take an S.G. reading and subtract from 1.097 or 1.114. Ferment as usual, making S.S.S. additions as necessary, finishing with an S.G. of 0.990–1.000. (The acidity of this wine may be rather too high—if so it may be reduced by the use of precipitated chalk according to instructions in Chapter V, p. 72).

GOOSEBERRY (2)
Wine style—Dry table wine (Hock type)

> 3×1 lb. 3 oz. (540 gm.) tins gooseberries
> 1 pint (568 ml.) Hock grape concentrate
> $\frac{3}{4}$ lb. (340 gm.) sugar as S.S.S.
> $\frac{1}{2}$ lb. (227 gm.) peeled over-ripe bananas
> 3 mg. vitamin B tablet
> Pectin destroying enzyme
> $\frac{1}{2}$ cup tea or 1/30 oz. (1 gm.) grape tannin
> All purpose or Hock yeast starter
> Yeast nutrient
> Water to make up the volume to 7 pints (4 litres)

Method

Use Method 1, Chapter VI.

Prepare as in Gooseberry (1). Ferment as usual, finishing with an S.G. of 0.990–1.000.

GOOSEBERRY (3)
Wine style—Dry white table wine

2 lb. (0.9 kilo) fresh gooseberries
½ pint (284 ml.) white grape concentrate
1¼ lb. (567 gm.) sugar as S.S.S.
½ lb. (227 gm.) peeled over-ripe bananas
3 mg. vitamin B tablet
1 Campden tablet or 5 ml. strong sulphite solution
Pectin destroying enzyme
All purpose or Hock yeast starter
Yeast nutrient
Water to make up the volume to 7 pints (4 litres)

Method

Use Method 1, Chapter VI.

Top and tail the gooseberries, crush them in a sterilised bucket and pour over 2 pints (1.14 litres) boiling water. Add grape concentrate and prepared banana 'gravy', cover, cool then add sulphite and pectin destroying enzyme. Leave covered 24 hours then add all other ingredients, mix well, take an S.G. reading and subtract from 1.097 or 1.114. Ferment as usual, making S.S.S. additions as necessary, finishing with an S.G. of 0.990–1.000.

GORSE (or broom)
Wine style—Medium dry social wine

4 pints (2.27 litres) gorse flowers
½ lb. (227 gm.) sultanas
2 lb. (0.9 kilo) sugar as S.S.S.
1 lemon
2 oranges
2, 3 mg. vitamin B tablets
Yeast energiser
1 Campden tablet or 5 ml. strong sulphite solution
Pectin destroying enzyme
½ cup tea or 1/30 oz. (1 gm.) grape tannin
All purpose yeast starter
Yeast nutrient
Water to make up the volume to 7 pints (4 litres)

Method

Use Method 1, Chapter VI.

Place the flowers in a bucket and pour over $2\frac{1}{2}$ pints (1.42 litres) boiling water. Add minced or liquidised sultanas plus the *finely* grated peel and the juice of the oranges and lemon. Cover, cool and add sulphite and pectin destroying enzyme. Leave covered 24 hours then add all other ingredients, mix well, take an S.G. reading and subtract from 1.114. Ferment as usual, making S.S.S. additions as necessary, finishing with an S.G. of 1.004–1.010.

GRAPE (1)

Wine style—White dry table wine

$5\frac{1}{2}$ lb. (2.5 kilos) white grapes
$1\frac{1}{4}$ lb. (567 gm.) sugar as S.S.S.
3 mg. vitamin B tablet
Pectin destroying enzyme
$\frac{1}{2}$ cup tea or 1/30 oz. (1 gm.) grape tannin
1 Campden tablet or 5 ml. strong sulphite solution
All purpose or Bordeaux yeast starter
Yeast nutrient
Water to make up the volume to 7 pints (4 litres)

Method

Use Method 1, Chapter VI.

Wash the fruit, place in a clean bucket and crush. Pour over 3 pints (1.7 litres) boiling water, cover, cool add sulphite and pectin destroying enzyme. Leave covered 24 hours then add all other ingredients (allow for approximately $2\frac{1}{2}$ pints (1.42 litres) of juice in the grapes), mix well, take an S.G. reading and subtract from 1.097 or 1.114. Ferment as usual, making S.S.S. additions as necessary, finishing with an S.G. of 0.990–1.000.

GRAPE (2)

Wine style—Red dry table wine

5 lb. (2.27 kilos) black dessert grapes
$1\frac{1}{4}$ lb. (567 gm.) sugar as S.S.S.
3 mg. vitamin B tablet
Pectin destroying enzyme
1 Campden tablet or 5 ml. strong sulphite solution
1 cup tea or 1/15 oz. (2 gm.) grape tannin
All purpose or Bordeaux yeast starter
Yeast nutrient
Water to make up the volume to 7 pints (4 litres)

Method

Use Method 1, Chapter VI.

Follow the procedures as for previous recipe.

GRAPEFRUIT (1)

Wine style—Dry white table wine

1 large tin (1.22 litres) unsweetened grapefruit juice
½ lb. (227 gm.) sultanas
1¾ lb. (794 gm.) sugar as S.S.S.
½ cup tea or 1/30 oz. (1 gm.) grape tannin
2, 3 mg. vitamin B tablets
1 Campden tablet or 5 ml. strong sulphite solution
Pectin destroying enzyme
All purpose or Burgundy yeast starter
Yeast nutrient
Water to make up the volume to 7 pints (4 litres)

Method

If the grapefruit juice contains preservative, simmer for three minutes to remove the excess. Into a clean bucket put the grapefruit juice and minced or liquidised sultanas, adding sulphite and pectin destroying enzyme. Leave covered 24 hours then add all other ingredients, mix well, take an S.G. reading and subtract from 1.097 or 1.114. Ferment as usual, making S.S.S. additions as necessary, finishing with an S.G. of 0.990–1.000. (The acidity may need to be reduced by the use of chalk.)

GPAPEFRUIT (2)

Wine style—Dry white table wine

1 large tin (1.22 litres) unsweetened grapefruit juice
½ pint (284 ml.) white grape concentrate
1 lb. (454 gm.) peeled over-ripe bananas
1¼ lb. (567 gm.) sugar as S.S.S.
2, 3 mg. vitamin B tablets
Pectin destroying enzyme
1 Campden tablet or 5 ml. strong sulphite solution
½ cup tea or 1/30 oz. (1 gm.) grape tannin
All purpose or Hock type yeast starter
Yeast nutrient
Water to make up the volume to 7 pints (4 litres)

Method

Use Method 3, Chapter VI.

If juice contains preservative, simmer for three minutes. Pour the grapefruit juice (cooled), grape concentrate, and prepared banana 'gravy' into a clean demijohn and add sulphite and pectin destroying enzyme. Cover the neck of the jar with a tissue and elastic band. Leave 24 hours then add all other recipe ingredients, mix well, take an S.G. reading and subtract from 1.097 or 1.114. Ferment as usual, making S.S.S. additions as necessary, finishing with an S.G. of 0.990–1.000. (The acidity may need to be reduced by the use of chalk.)

GRAPEFRUIT (3)
Wine style—Dry aperitif

9 large grapefruit
½ pint (284 ml.) white grape concentrate
½ lb. (227 gm.) sultanas
1½ lb. (680 gm.) sugar as S.S.S.
2, 3 mg. vitamin B tablets
Pectin destroying enzyme
1 cup tea or 1/15 oz. (2 gm.) grape tannin
All purpose yeast starter
Yeast nutreint
Water to make up the volume to 7 pints (4 litres)

Method

Peel the grapefruit carefully, removing as much pith as possible. Discard the peel. Chop up the segments and place in a fine mesh straining bag—squeeze out the juice into a receiving vessel, then pour 2 pints (1.14 litres) boiling water through the pulp and squeeze again when cool. Discard the pulp. Measure the volume of grapefruit juice obtained and transfer it into a clean bucket, together with the grape contrate and minced or liquidised sultanas. Add sulphite and pectin destroying enzyme when cool. Leave covered 24 hours then add all other ingredients, mix well, take an S.G. reading and subtract from 1.148, as this wine requires to be high in alcohol. Ferment as usual, making S.S.S. additions as necessary, being careful to allow the S.G. to drop to 0.990 before each addition, particularly when the fermentation is slowing down. Stop adding S.S.S. when the fermentation becomes very sluggish and allow to ferment out to 0.990–0.994. It will be unlikely that *all* the extra S.S.S. can be added and a dry wine still be obtained. (Since the high alcohol content masks the presence of residual sugar, a reading of 0.990 on the hydrometer does not necessarily mean that the wine tastes dry.) Tasting the wine between each S.S.S. addition will be of help to ascertain when to stop S.S.S. additions. If some residual sugar can be detected—DO NOT ADD MORE S.S.S. until that present has been utilised by the yeast.

GRAPEFRUIT (4)
Wine style—Medium social wine
1 bottle Quosh grapefruit and pineapple
½ lb. (227 gm.) sultanas
1¾ lb. (794 gm.) sugar as S.S.S.
2, 3 mg. vitamin B tablets
Pectin destroying enzyme
1 Campden tablet or 5 ml. strong sulphite solution
¼ cup tea or 1/30 oz. (1 gm.) grape tannin
All purpose yeast starter
Yeast nutrient
Water to make up the volume to 7 pints (4 litres)

Method

Use Method 2, Chapter VI.

Simmer the cordial for three minutes to remove excess preservative. Pour the cooled juice into a clean bucket, add the minced or liquidised sultanas and add sulphite and pectin destroying enzyme. Leave covered 24 hours then add all other ingredients, mix well, take an S.G. reading and subtract from 1.131. Ferment as usual, making S.S.S. additions as necessary, finishing with an S.G. of 1.010.

GUAVA and BANANA (Guavanana)
Wine style—Sweet white wine
By courtesy of Mr. B. C. Campbell—Tynemouth Winemaking Society
3 × 15½ oz. (3 × 439 gm.) tins Guavas
6 oz. (170 gm.) dried bananas
2 teaspoons citric acid
1 teaspoon tannin
1 teaspoon Tronozymol nutrient
1 teaspoon pectin destroying enzyme
1 sachet all purpose yeast
3 lb. (1.36 kilos) sugar

Method

Chop the bananas finely and put into a pan with 2 pints (1.14 litres) of hot water. When soft, bring to the boil and simmer for 20 minutes. Meanwhile, put the guavas and 2 lb. sugar into the bucket and stir well, crushing the guavas. Empty the bananas and liquid into the bucket, add 1 pint (568 ml.) cold water, stir, cover and allow to cool. Add pectin destroying enzyme, acid, tannin, nutrient and yeast, again stir well. Cover and ferment on the pulp for four days then strain into a demijohn. Fit air lock. After seven days add the remaining 1 lb. (454 gm.) sugar (in syrup form) and top up to the neck with cold water. Mix thoroughly at this stage. When fermentation ceases, rack and add one soluble Campden tablet. Repeat this two months later and after another month the wine should be ready for bottling.

HAWTHORN BLOSSOM (May blossom)
Wine style—Dry table or social wine
4 pints (2.27 litres) blossom
½ lb. (227 gm.) sultanas
1¾ lb. (794 gm.) sugar as S.S.S.
2 lemons
¼ cup tea or 1/30 oz. (1 gm.) grape tannin
2, 3 mg. vitamin B tablets
1 Campden tablet or 5 ml. strong sulphite solution
Pectin destroying enzyme
All purpose or Bordeaux yeast starter
Yeast nutrient
Yeast energiser
Water to make up the volume to 7 pints (4 litres)

Method

Use Method 1, Chapter VI.

Cut the flowers from the stems with scissors and place in a clean bucket. Add the minced or liquidised sultanas, the finely grated peel and juice of the lemons and 3 pints (1.7 litres) boiling water. Cover, cool and add sulphite and pectin destroying enzyme. Leave covered 24 hours then add all other ingredients, mix well, take an S.G. reading and subtract from 1.097 to 1.114. Ferment as ususal, making S.S.S. additions as necessary, finishing with an S.G. of 0.990–1.000.

HAWTHORN BLOSSOM (2)
Wine style—Medium sweet social wine
4 pints (2.27 litres) blossom
½ lb. (227 gm.) sultanas or currants
1 lb. (454 gm.) peeled over-ripe bananas
2 lb. (0.9 kilo) sugar as S.S.S.
2, 3 mg. vitamin B tablets
Pectin destroying enzyme
1 cup tea or 1/15 oz. (2 gm.) tannin
2 oranges
All purpose or Bordeaux yeast starter
Yeast nutrient
Yeast energiser
1 Campden tablet or 5 ml. strong sulphite solution
Water to make up the volume to 7 pints (4 litres)

Method

Use Method 1, Chapter VI.

Cut the blossoms from the stems and put them in a clean bucket together with the minced or liquidised dried fruit, the finely grated peel and juice of the oranges and the prepared banana 'gravy'. Pour over 2½ pints (1.42 litres) boiling water. Cover, cool and add sulphite and pectin destroying enzyme. Leave covered 24 hours then add all other ingredients, mix well, take an S.G. reading and subtract from 1.131. Ferment as usual, making S.S.S additions as necessary, finishing with an S.G. of 1.006–1.014.

HONEYSUCKLE (1)

Wine style—Medium dry social wine

2½ pints (1.42 litres) honeysuckle flowers (preferably wild)

½ lb. (227 gm.) sultanas

2 lb. (0.9 kilo) sugar as S.S.S.

2, 3 mg. vitamin B tablets

Pectin destroying enzyme

1 Campden tablet or 5 ml. strong sulphite solution

½ cup tea or 1/30 oz. (1 gm.) grape tannin

¼ oz. (7 gm.) citric or mixed acids

All purpose or Bordeaux yeast starter

Yeast nutrient

Yeast energiser

Water to make up the volume to 7 pints (4 litres)

Method

Use Method 1, Chapter VI.

Pour 2 pints (1.14 litres) boiling water over the flowers in a clean bucket and add the minced or liquidised sultanas. Cover, cool and add sulphite and pectin destroying enzyme. Leave covered 24 hours then add all other ingredients, mix well, take an S.G. reading and subtract from 1.114. Ferment as usual, making S.S.S. additions as necessary, finishing with an S.G. of 1.004–1.010.

HONEYSUCKLE (2)

Wine style—Medium sweet social wine

3 pints (1.7 litres) honeysuckle flowers (preferably wild)
½ pint (284 ml.) white grape concentrate
1¾ lb. (794 gm.) sugar as S.S.S.
2, 3 mg. vitamin B tablets
Pectin destroying enzyme
1 Campden tablet or 5 ml. strong sulphite solution
⅜ oz. (11 gm.) acid mixture or ¼ oz. (7 gm.) citric acid
½ cup tea or 1/30 oz. (1 gm.) grape tannin
All purpose or Bordeaux yeast starter
Yeast nutrient
Yeast energiser
Water to make up the volume to 7 pints (4 litres)

Method

Use Method 1, Chapter VI.

Prepare the must as in Honeysuckle (1) adding the grape concentrate instead of the sultanas. Subtract the S.G. from 1.131. Ferment as usual, making S.S.S. additions as necessary, finishing with an S.G. of 1.006–1.014.

HONEYSUCKLE (3)

Wine style—Sweet social wine

3 pints (1.7 litres) honeysuckle flowers (preferably wild)
¾ lb. (340 gm.) raisins or currants
2 lb. 2 oz. (964 gm.) sugar as S.S.S.
2, 3 mg. vitamin B tablets
Pectin destroying enzyme
1 Campden tablet or 5 ml. strong sulphite solution
¼ oz. (7 gm.) mixed acids or citric acid
½ cup tea or 1/30 oz. (1 gm.) grape tannin
All purpose or Sauternes yeast starter
Yeast nutrient
Yeast energiser
Water to make up the volume to 7 pints (4 litres)

Method

Use Method 1, Chapter VI.

Prepare the must as in previous recipes, subtracting the S.G. from 1.148. Ferment as usual, making S.S.S. additions as necessary, finishing with an S.G. of 1.020.

HONEYSUCKLE (4)

Wine style—Medium sweet social wine

2 pints (1.14 litres) honeysuckle flowers (preferably wild)
2 pints (1.14 litres) scented rose petals
¾ lb. (340 gm.) currants
2 lb. (0.9 kilo) sugar as S.S.S.
2, 3 mg. vitamin B tablets
Pectin destroying enzyme
1 Campden tablet or 5 ml. strong sulphite solution
½ cup tea or 1/30 oz. (1 gm.) grape tannin
¼ oz. (7 gm.) citric or acid mixture
All purpose or Sauternes yeast starter
Yeast nutrient
Yeast energiser
Water to make up the volume to 7 pints (4 litres)

Method

Use Method 1, Chapter VI.

Put the flowers in a clean bucket and prepare the must as usual, (see Honeysuckle (1)) subtracting the S.G. from 1.131. Proceed as usual, finishing with an S.G. of 1.010–1.014.

LEMON BALM (Lemon mint)

Wine style—Medium dry social wine

1½ pints (852 ml.) lemon balm leaves
½ lb. (227 gm.) sultanas
2 lb. (0.9 kilos) sugar as S.S.S.
2, 3 mg. vitamin B tablets
Pectin destroying enzyme
1 Campden tablet or 5 ml. strong sulphite solution
½ cup tea or 1/30 oz. (1 gm.) grape tannin
¼ oz. (7 gm.) citric or mixed acids
All purpose yeast starter
Yeast nutrient
Yeast energiser
Water to make up the volume to 7 pints (4 litres)

Method

Use Method 1, Chapter VI.

Prepare the must as in Honeysuckle (1) subtracting the S.G. from 1.131. Ferment as usual, making S.S.S. additions as necessary, finishing with an S.G. of 1.004–1.010.

LIME (1)
Wine style—Medium social wine
1 large bottle lime juice cordial
½ lb. (227 gm.) sultanas
1¾ lb. (794 gm.) sugar as S.S.S.
2, 3 mg. vitamin B tablets
½ cup tea or 1/30 oz. (1 gm.) grape tannin
Pectin destroying enzyme
All purpose yeast starter
Yeast nutrient
Yeast energiser
Water to make up the volume to 7 pints (4 litres)

Method

Use Method 1, Chapter VI.

Empty the lime juice into a pan and simmer for three minutes to remove excess preservative, then pour it into a clean bucket with the minced or liquidised sultanas. Cover, cool and add sulphite and pectin destroying enzyme. Leave covered 24 hours then add all other ingredients, mix well, take an S.G. reading and subtract from 1.131. Ferment as usual, making S.S.S. additions as necessary, finishing with an S.G. of 1.010–1.014. (The acidity of this wine may have to be reduced to taste by the use of precipitated chalk.)

LIME (2)
Wine style—Sweet social or Sauternes type wine
1 large bottle lime juice cordial
½ lb. (227 gm.) sultanas
1 lb. (454 gm.) over-ripe bananas (peeled plus 3 skins)
½ pint (284 ml.) white grape concentrate
1¼ lb. (567 gm.) sugar as S.S.S.
2, 3 mg. vitamin B tablets
1 Campden tablet or 5 ml. strong sulphite solution
½ cup tea or 1/30 oz. (1 gm.) grape tannin
Pectin destroying enzyme
All purpose or Sauternes yeast starter
Yeast nutrient
Yeast energiser
Water to make up the volume to 7 pints (4 litres)

Method

Use Method 1, Chapter VI.

Simmer the lime juice for three minutes to remove excess preservative, then pour it into a clean bucket together with the minced or liquidised sultanas, grape concentrate and prepared banana 'gravy'. Cover, cool then add sulphite and pectin

180

destroying enzyme. Leave covered 24 hours then add all other ingredients, mix well, take an S.G. reading and subtract from 1.148. Ferment as usual making S.S.S. additions as necessary, finishing with an S.G. of 1.020. .

MARROW
Wine style—medium social wine

5 lb. (2.27 kilos) marrow
2¼ lb. (1.02 kilos) sugar as S.S.S.
2 lemons
1 orange
½ oz. (14 gm.) root ginger
1 cup tea or 1/15 oz. (2 gm.) grape tannin
3 mg. vitamin B tablet
1 Campden tablet or 5 ml. strong sulphite solution
Pectin destroying enzyme
All purpose yeast starter
Yeast nutrient
Water to make up the volume to 7 pints (4 litres)

Method

Use Method 1, Chapter VI.

Grate or chop up the marrow including skin but discard the seeds. Put the marrow into a clean bucket together with the finely grated peel and juice of the lemons and orange. Crush the ginger with a mallet and add it to the bucket. Pour over 2 pints (1.14 litres) boiling water. (Remember that the marrow will yield approximately 2 pints (1.14 litres) juice). Cover, cool and add sulphite and pectin destroying enzyme. Leave covered 24 hours then add all other ingredients, mix well, take an S.G. reading and subtract from 1.131. Ferment as usual, making S.S.S. additions as necessary, finishing with an S.G. of 1.004–1.010.

NETTLE
Wine style—Medium social wine

4 pints (2.27 litres) young nettle tops
½ lb. (227 gm.) sultanas
2 lb. (0.9 kilo) sugar as S.S.S.
2 lemons
½ oz. (14 gm.) root ginger
2, 3 mg. vitamin B tablets
Pectin destroying enzyme
½ cup tea or 1/30 oz. (1 gm.) grape tannin
1 Campden tablet or 5 ml. strong sulphite solution
All purpose yeast starter
Yeast nutrient
Yeast energiser
Water to make up the volume to 7 pints (4 litres)

Method

Use Method 1, Chapter VI.

Place the nettles in a clean bucket together with the finely grated peel and juice of the lemons and the minced or liquidised sultanas. Pour over 3 pints (1.7 litres) boiling water, cover, cool and add sulphite and pectin destroying enzyme. Leave 24 hours then add all other ingredients, mix well, take an S.G. reading and subtract from 1.131. Ferment as usual, making S.S.S. additions as necessary, finishing with an S.G. of 1.006–1.014.

ORANGE (1)
Wine style—Dry aperitif

1 large can (1.22 litres) pure unsweetened orange juice
1 pint (568 ml.) white grape concentrate
3 mg. vitamin B tablet
1 lb. (454 gm.) sugar as S.S.S.
1 cup tea or 1/15 oz. (2 gm.) grape tannin
Pectin destroying enzyme
All purpose or Sauternes yeast starter
Yeast nutrient
Water to make up the volume to 7 pints (4 litres)

Method

If the orange juice contains preservative, simmer for three minutes to remove the excess. Cool and pour into a clean demijohn. Add all other ingredients, mix well, take an S.G. reading and subtract from 1.148. Cover the neck of the jar with a tissue and elastic band and ferment as usual making carefully controlled S.S.S. additions as in Grapefruit (3). The final S.G. should be 0.990–0.994. The acidity may have to be reduced by the use of precipitated chalk. If titration for acid is being done, the acidity required is 5 p.p.t. as sulphuric acid.

ORANGE (2)
Wine style—Dry aperitif

By courtesy of Mr. T. D. Hodkinson—Tynemouth Winemaking Society

3rd. Prize—Dry aperitif class—N.Y. & S.D. Show 1976

2 lb. (0.9 kilo) Seville oranges
1 pint (568 ml.) white grape concentrate
1 lb. (454 gm.) sugar as S.S.S.
3 mg. vitamin B tablet
1 Campden tablet or 5 ml. strong sulphite solution
Pectin destroying enzyme
All purpose yeast starter
Yeast nutrient
Water to make up the volume to 7 pints (4 litres)

A sweet version of this wine won 2nd Prize N.Y. & S.D. Show 1977

Method

Wash and peel the oranges carefully avoiding the pith. Boil the peel for five minutes in 1 pint (568 ml.) water. Leave covered for 24 hours. Squeeze and strain the juice from the oranges, measure the volume and pour into a clean demijohn. Add the grape concentrate, nutrients, vitamin B tablet, pectin destroying enzyme and yeast starter, and make up to 5 pints (2.84 litres) with water. Fit an air-lock and stand in a warm place, After 24 hours add the strained liquor from the peel. When fermentation slows down, check S.G. and if below 1.010 add 1 lb. (454 gm.) sugar in syrup form. Thereafter when the S.G. falls below 1.005 add 227 gm. ($\frac{1}{2}$ lb.) sugar as syrup, then finally $\frac{1}{4}$ lb. (113 gm.) sugar, diluting with each addition, until with the final addition, the volume is 1 gallon (4.5 litres). Ferment to dryness—0.990.

ORANGE (3)
Wine style—Dry apertif
1 large can (1.22 litres) pure unsweetened orange juice
$\frac{3}{4}$ lb. (340 gm.) sultanas
1 lb. (454 gm.) peeled over-ripe bananas
1$\frac{3}{4}$ lb. (794 gm.) sugar as S.S.S.
4 oranges
2, 3 mg. vitamin B tablet
Pectin destroying enzyme
1 Campden tablet or 5 ml. strong strong sulphite
All purpose or Sauternes yeast starter
Yeast nutrient
Water to make up the volume to 7 pints (4 litres)

Method

If the fruit juice contains preservative, simmer for three minutes to remove the excess, then put it into a sterilised bucket together with the minced or liquidised sultanas, the finely grated peel of the oranges and the prepared banana 'gravy'. Cover, cool and add sulphite and pectin destroying enzyme. Leave covered 24 hours then add all other ingredients, mix well, take an S.G. reading and subtract from 1.148. Proceed as described in Grapefruit (3), finishing with an S.G. of 0.990–0.994. (The acidity of this wine may have to be reduced by the use of chalk. The acidity should be about 5 p.p.t. sulphuric acid.)

ORANGE (4)
Wine style—Medium dry social wine
8 medium sized oranges
½ lb. (227 gm.) raisins
2 lb. (0.9 kilo) sugar as S.S.S.
2, 3 mg. vitamin B tablets
1 Campden tablet or 5 ml. strong sulphite solution
Pectin destroying enzyme
½ cup tea or 1/30 oz. (1 gm.) grape tannin
All purpose or Bordeaux yeast starter
Yeast nutrient
Yeast energiser
Water to make up the volume to 7 pints (4 litres)

Method

Finely grate the peel of six of the oranges, simmer in ½ pint (284 ml.) water for five minutes, and leave to infuse over-night. Squeeze the juice from all the oranges, strain, measure the volume and pour into a clean bucket. Add minced or liquidised raisins and 2 pints (1.14 litres) boiling water. Cover, cool and add sulphite and pectin destroying enzyme. Cover and leave 24 hours then add all other ingredients, mix well, take an S.G. reading and subtract from 1.131. Ferment as usual, making S.S.S. additions as usual, finishing with an S.G. of 1.004–1.010. (This wine may be rather slow to ferment due to the inhibitive effect on the yeast of the peel extract.)

ORANGE (5)
Wine style—Sweet social or Sauternes type wine
3rd Prize Fruit—white sweet—citrus—National 1977

1 large can (1.22 litres) unsweetened pure orange juice
½ pint (284 ml.) white grape concentrate
1 lb. (454 gm.) peeled over-ripe bananas plus skins
3 mg. vitamin B tablet
1½ lb. (680 gm.) sugar as S.S.S.
1 cup tea or 1/15 oz. (2 gm.) grape tannin
1 Campden tablet or 5 ml. strong sulphite solution
Pectin destroying enzyme
All purpose or Sauternes yeast starter
Yeast nutrient
Water to make up the volume to 4 pints (7 litres)

Method

Simmer the orange juice for three minutes, if known to contain preservative. Pour the cool juice into a clean demijohn together with the grape concentrate and prepared banana

184

'gravy'. Add sulphite and pectin destroying enzyme, cover the neck of the jar and leave 24 hours. Next day add all the other ingredients, mix well, take an S.G. reading and subtract from 1.148. Ferment as usual, making S.S.S. additions as necessary, finishing with an S.G. of 1.020. The acidity of this wine may have to be reduced by the use of chalk.

ORANGE (6)
Wine style—Medium sweet social wine
19 fl. oz. (540 ml.) can pure unsweetened orange juice
19 fl. oz. (540 ml.) can pure unsweetened pineapple juice
½ pint (284 ml.) white grape concentrate
1½ lb. (680 gm.) sugar as S.S.S.
3 mg. vitamin B tablet
1 cup tea or 1/15 oz. (2 gm.) grape tannin
Pectin destroying enzyme
All purpose or Sauternes yeast starter
Yeast nutrient
Water to make up the volume to 7 pints (4 litres)

Method

Prepare as in Orange (5) omitting the banana 'gravy'. Subtract the S.G. from 1.131. The final S.G. should be 1.006–1.014.

PEACH (1)
Wine style—Dry table wine
2 family sized tins peaches (820 gm. size)
½ lb. (227 gm.) sultanas
1¼ lb. (567 gm.) sugar as S.S.S.
2, 3 mg. vitamin B tablets
Pectin destroying enzyme
¼ oz. (7 gm.) citric or mixed acid
½ cup tea or 1/30 oz. (1 gm.) grape tannin
All purpose or Sauternes yeast starter
Yeast nutrient
Water to make up the volume to 7 pints (4 litres)

Method

Use Method 1, Chapter VI.

Strain the syrup from the peaches and measure the volume. Put the peaches into a clean bucket and crush, then add the minced or liquidised sultanas, peach syrup and all other ingredients. Mix well, take an S.G. reading and subtract from 0.097 or 1.114. Ferment as usual, making S.S.S. additions as necessary, finishing with an S.G. or 0.990–1.000.

185

PEACH (2)
Wine style—Dry white table wine
4 lb. (1.8 kilos) ripe peaches
½ pint (284 ml.) white grape concentrate
1¼ lb. (567 gm.) sugar as S.S.S.
½ lb. (227 gm.) peeled over-ripe bananas
3 mg. vitamin B tablet
¼ oz. (7 gm.) citric or mixed acid
Yeast nutreint
1 Campden tablet or 5 ml. strong sulphite solution
Pectin destroying enzyme
½ cup tea or 1/30 oz. (1 gm.) grape tannin
All purpose or Bordeaux yeast starter
Water to make up the volume to 7 pints (4 litres)

Method

Use Method 1, Chapter VI.

Wash and stone the peaches and crush in a clean bucket, adding the grape concentrate, prepared banana 'gravy' and 2 pints (1.14 litres) boiling water. Cover, cool and add sulphite and pectin destroying enzyme, Leave covered 24 hours, then add all other ingredients, mix well, take an S.G. reading and subtract from 1.097 or 1.114. Ferment as usual, making S.S.S. additions as necessary, finishing with an S.G. of 0.990–1.000.

PEACH (3)
Wine style—Sweet social or Sauternes type wine
6 lb. (2.72 kilos) ripe peaches
½ pint (284 ml.) white grape concentrate
   (preferably Sauternes type)
½ lb. (227 gm.) sultanas
1¼ lb. (557 gm.) sugar as S.S.S.
3 mg. vitamin B tablet
1 Campden tablet or 5 ml. strong sulphite solution
Pectin destroying enzyme
All purpose or Sauternes yeast starter
Yeast nutrient
Water to make up the volume to 7 pints (4 litres)

Method

Use Method 1, Chapter VI.

Wash and stone the peaches and crush in a clean bucket, add the minced or liquidised sultanas, grape concentrate and 2 pints (1.14 litres) boiling water, Cover, cool and add sulphite and pectin destroying enzyme then leave covered 24 hours. Next day add all other ingredients (allow for 2 pints (1.14 litres) juice in the peaches), mix well, take an S.G. reading and subtract from 1.148. Ferment as usual making S.S.S. additions as necessary, finishing with an S.G. of 1.020.

PEA-POD
Wine style—Dry table wine

The peas may be blanched and stored for future use in the freezer.

      5 lb. (2.27 kilos) pea-pods
      $\frac{1}{2}$ lb. (227 gm.) sultanas
      1$\frac{3}{4}$ lb. (794 gm.) sugar as S.S.S.
      2, 3 mg. vitamin B tablets
      Pectin destroying enzyme
      $\frac{1}{4}$ oz. (7 gm.) citric acid or mixed acid
      $\frac{1}{2}$ cup of tea or 1/30 oz. (1 gm.) grape tannin
      All purpose or Bordeaux yeast starter
      Yeast nutrient
      Water to make up the volume to 7 pints (4 litres)

Method

Use Method 3, Chapter VI.

Put the washed pea-pods and minced or liquidised sultanas into a pan containing 3 pints (1.7 litres) boiling water and simmer for $\frac{1}{2}$ hour. Strain through a seive or nylon straining bag and allow the liquor to cool. Discard the pulp. When the liquor is cool, measure the volume and pour into a clean demijohn, adding all the other ingredients, mix well, take an S.G. reading and subtract from 1.097 or 1.114. Ferment as usual, making S.S.S. additions as necessary, finishing with an S.G. of 0.990–1.000.

PEAR (1)
Wine style—Dry white table wine

      4 lb. (1.8 kilos) ripe pears
      $\frac{1}{4}$ lb. (113 gm.) sultanas
      1$\frac{1}{2}$ lb. (680 gm.) sugar as S.S.S.
      3 mg. vitamin B tablet
      Pectin destroying enzyme
      $\frac{3}{8}$ oz. (11 gm.) mixed acids or $\frac{1}{4}$ oz. (7 gm.) citric acid
      1 Campden tablet or 5ml. strong sulphite solution
      All purpose or Bordeaux yeast starter
      Yeast nutrient
      Water to make up the volume to 7 pints (4 litres)

Method

Use Method 2, Chapter VI.

Peel all but 4–6 of the pears (depending on size) and discard these peelings. Chop each piece of fruit into small chunks and put it quickly into a bucket containing 2$\frac{1}{2}$ pints (1.42 litres) of cold water to which the sulphite has already been added.

(This will prevent oxidative browning of the fruit.) Add the minced or liquidised sultanas, cover and leave 24 hours. Next day add all other ingredients, mix well, take an S.G. reading and subtract from 1.097 or 1.114. Ferment as usual, making S.S.S. additions as necessary, finishing with an S.G. of 0.990–1.000.

PEAR (2)
Wine style—Dry white table wine
3rd Prize—Fruit—white dry class—National 1976

> 4 lb. (1.8 kilos) ripe pears
> ½ pint (284 ml.) white grape concentrate
> 1¼ lb. (567 gm.) sugar as S.S.S.
> 3 mg. vitamin B tablet
> Pectin destroying enzyme
> ¼ oz. (7 gm.) citric acid mixture
> 1 Campden tablet or 5 ml. strong sulphite solution
> All purpose or Burgundy yeast starter
> Yeast nutrient
> Water to make up the volume to 7 pints (4 litres)

Method

Use Method 2, Chapter VI

Prepare the pears as in the previous recipe. Add grape concentrate and after leaving covered 24 hours, add all other ingredients, mix well, take an S.G. reading and subtract from 1.097 or 1.114. Proceed as usual, finishing with an S.G. of 0.990–1.000.

PEAR (3)
Wine style—Dry table wine

> 4 lb. (1.8 kilos) ripe pears
> 1 lb. (454 gm.) peeled over-ripe bananas
> 1¾ lb. (794 gm.) sugar as S.S.S.
> 3 mg. vitamin B tablet
> Pectin destroying enzyme
> ¼ oz. (7 gm.) citric or mixed acids
> 1 Campden tablet or 5 ml. strong sulphite solution
> All purpose or Bordeaux yeast starter
> Yeast nutrient
> Water to make up the volume to 7 pints (4 litres)

Method

Use Method 2, Chapter VI.

Prepare the pears as in Pear (1) and add the prepared banana 'gravy'. Leave covered 24 hours then add all other ingredients and continue as in Pear (1).

188

PEAR (4)

Wine style—Medium table wine

4 lb. (1.8 kilos) ripe pears
¾ pint (426 ml.) white grape concentrate
½ lb. (227 gm.) peeled over-ripe bananas
1¼ lb. (567 gm.) sugar as S.S.S.
All purpose or Leibfraumilch yeast starter
Yeast nutrient
3 mg. vitamin B tablet
Pectin destroying enzyme
1 Campden tablet or 5 ml. strong sulphite solution
Water to make up the volume to 7 pints (4 litres)

Method

Use Method 2, Chapter VI.

Prepare the pears as in Pear (1) and add the grape concentrate and prepared banana 'gravy'. Leave covered 24 hours, then proceed as in Pear (1), subtracting the S.G. from 1.114. Finish with an S.G. of 1.004–1.010.

This wine may be sweetened a little more for use as a sweet social wine if desired.

PINEAPPLE (1)

Wine style—Medium social wine

1 large tin (1.22 litres) pineapple juice
½ lb. (227 gm.) sultanas
1½ lb. (680 gm.) sugar as S.S.S.
3 mg. vitamin B tablet
Yeast nutrient
Pectin destroying enzyme
½ cup tea or 1/30 oz. (1 gm.) grape tannin
All purpose or Bordeaux yeast starter
Water to make up the volume to 7 pints (4 litres)

Method

Use Method 1, Chapter VI.

If the juice contains preservative, simmer for three minutes to remove the excess. Pour the juice (cooled) into a clean bucket and add the minced or liquidised sultanas and all other ingredients. Mix well, take an S.G. reading and subtract from 1.131. Ferment as usual, making S.S.S. additions as necessary, finishing with an S.G. of 1.006–1.014.

PINEAPPLE (2)
Wine style—Medium social wine
1 bottle Quosh pineapple and grapefruit cordial
½ lb. (227 gm.) sultanas
1¾ lb. (794 gm.) sugar as S.S.S.
2, 3 mg. vitamin B tablets
Pectin destroying enzyme
¼ cup tea or 1/30 oz. (1 gm.) grape tannin
All purpose or Bordeaux yeast starter
Yeast nutrient
Yeast energiser
Water to make up the volume to 7 pints (4 litres)

Method

Use Method 1, Chapter VI.

Simmer the cordial for three minutes to remove excess preservative, then cool and pour into a clean bucket. Add the minced or liquidised sultanas and all other ingredients, mix well, take an S.G. reading and subtract from 1.131. Ferment as usual, making S.S.S. additions as necessary, finishing with an S.G. of 1.006–1.014.

PINEAPPLE (3)
Wine style—Sweet social or dessert wine
1 large tin (1.22 litres) pineapple juice
½ pint (284 ml.) white grape concentrate
2 lb. (0.9 kilo) peeled over-ripe bananas plus ½ lb. (227 gm.) skins
1¼ lb. (567 gm.) sugar as S.S.S.
3 mg. vitamin B tablets
Pectin destroying enzyme
¼ cup tea or 1/30 oz. (1 gm.) grape tannin
All purpose or Sauternes yeast starter
Yeast nutrient
Water to make up the volume to 7 pints (4 litres)

Method

Compare Method 3, Chapter VI.

If the juice contains preservative, simmer for three minutes to remove the excess. When cool, pour the juice into a clean demijohn. Add the grape concentrate, prepared banana 'gravy' and all other ingredients, mix well, take an S.G. reading, and subtract from 1.148. Cover the neck of the jar with a tissue and ferment as usual, making S.S.S. additions as necessary, finishing with an S.G. of 1.020.

PRUNE
Wine style—Medium social wine

1 lb. (454 gm.) packet prunes
1¾ lb. (794 gm.) sugar as S.S.S.
2, 3 mg. vitamin B tablet
Pectin destroying enzyme
½ cup tea or 1/30 oz. (1 gm.) grape tannin
All purpose, Sherry or Tokay yeast starter
Yeast nutrient
Water to make up the volume to 7 pints (4 litres)

Method

Use Method 3, Chapter VI.

Either boil the prunes in 2 pints (1.14 litres) of water in an open pan for 20 minutes, or pressure-cook (at 15 lb. (6.8 kilos) pressure) in 1 pint (568 ml.) of water for five minutes. The fruit will now be soft and should be crushed and cooked again for the same length of time, with a little more water added. Strain off the pulp and discard it When cool, pour the liquor into a clean demijohn and add all other ingredients, mix well, take an S.G. reading and subtract from 1.131. Cover the neck of the jar with a tissue and ferment as usual, making S.S.S. additions as necessary, finishing with an S.G. of 1.006–1.014.

RAISIN (1)
Wine style—Medium social wine

1 lb. (454 gm.) raisins
1¾ lb. (794 gm.) sugar as S.S.S.
3 mg. vitamin B tablet
Pectin destroying enzyme
All purpose, Sherry or Madeira yeast starter
Yeast nutrient
Water to make up the volume to 7 pints (4 litres)

Method

Use Method 3, Chapter VI

Mince or liquidise the raisins and simmer in 3 pints (1.7 litres) water for 45 minutes to 1 hour or, pressure cook in 1 pint (568 ml.) water for 10–15 minutes at 15 lb. (6.8 kilos) pressure. Strain off the pulp and discard it. When cool, pour liquor into a clean demijohn and proceed as in the previous recipe, subtracting the S.G. from 1.131. Ferment as usual, making S.S.S. additions as necessary, finishsing with an S.G. of 1.006–1.014.

RAISIN (2)

Wine style—Sweet social wine

1½ lb. (680 gm.) raisins
1¾ lb. (794 gm.) sugar as S.S.S.
1 lb. (454 gm.) peeled over-ripe bananas
3 mg. vitamin B tablet
Pectin destroying enzyme
All purpose, Sherry or Madeira yeast starter
Yeast nutrient
Water to make up the volume to 7 pints (4 litres)

Method

Use Method 3, Chapter VI.

Prepare the raisins as in the previous recipe, strain off the pulp and when cool, pour the liquor into a clean demijohn. Add the prepared banana 'gravy' when cooled and all the other ingredients, mix well, take an S.G. reading and subtract from 1.148. Ferment as usual, making S.S.S. additions as necessary, finishing with an S.G. of 1.020.

RASPBERRY (1)

Wine style—Medium social wine

1 bottle Quosh raspberry cordial
1 lb. (454 gm.) peeled over-ripe bananas
1½ lb. (680 gm.) sugar as S.S.S.
2, 3 mg. vitamin B tablets
Yeast energiser
Pectin destroying enzyme
1 cup tea or 1/15 oz. (2 gm.) grape tannin
All purpose yeast starter
Yeast nutrient
Water to make up the volume to 7 pints (4 litres)

Method

Use Method 3, Chapter VI.

Simmer the raspberry cordial for three minutes to remove excess preservative. Cool and pour into a clean demijohn. adding the prepared banana 'gravy' and all other ingredients. Mix well, take an S.G. reading and subtract from 1.131. Ferment as usual, making S.S.S. additions as necessary, finishing with an S.G. of 1.006–1.014. The pink colour of this wine disappears during maturation, leaving it a golden colour.

RASPBERRY (2)
Wine style—Medium social wine
3 lb. (1.36 kilos) raspberries
½ lb. (227 gm.) sultanas
1¾ lb. (794 gm.) sugar as S.S.S.
3 mg. vitamin B tablet
Pectin destroying enzyme
1 Campden tablet or 5 ml. strong sulphite solution
½ cup tea or 1/30 oz. (1 gm.) grape tannin
All purpose yeast starter
Yeast nutrient
Water to make up the volume to 7 pints (4 litres)

Method

Use Method 1, Chapter VI.

Wash the raspberries then crush them in a sterilised bucket. Add the minced or liquidised sultanas and 2½ pints (1.42 litres) boiling water. Cover, cool and add sulphite and pectin destroying enzyme. Leave covered 24 hours then add all other ingredients, mix well, take an S.G. reading and subtract from 1.131. Ferment as usual, making S.S.S. additions as necessary, finishing with an S.G. of 1.006–1.014.

RICE
Wine style—Medium social wine
2 lb. (0.9 kilo) long grain or brown rice
½ lb. (227 gm.) raisins
2 lb. (0.9 kilo) sugar as S.S.S.
3 mg. vitamin B tablet
Pectin destroying enzyme
¼ oz. (7 gm.) citric acid or acid mixture
½ cup tea or 1/30 oz. (1 gm.) grape tannin
All purpose yeast starter
Yeast nutrient
Water to make up the volume to 7 pints (4 litres)

Method

Use Method 1, Chapter VI.

Put the rice and the minced or liquidised raisins into a clean bucket and pour over 3 pints (1.7 litres) boiling water. Cover, cool and add sulphite and pectin destroying enzyme. Leave covered 24 hours then add all other ingredients, mix well, take an S.G. reading and subtract from 1.131. Ferment as usual, making S.S.S. additions as necessary, finishing with an S.G. of 1.006–1.010.

This wine is very harsh when young and consequently requires about 2 years maturation.

ROSEHIP (1)
Wine style—Medium dry social wine
2½ lb. (1.13 kilos) fresh rosehips
½ lb. (227 gm.) peeled over-ripe bananas (optional)
1¾ lb. (794 gm.) sugar as S.S.S.
Pectin destroying enzyme
1 Campden tablet or 5 ml. strong sulphite solution
All purpose or Sherry yeast starter
Yeast nutrient
Water to make up the volume to 7 pints (4 litres)

Method

Crush the rosehips in a clean bucket. (If the hips are too hard to crush, mince or liquidise them, or simmer them for 10–15 minutes in 2–3 pints (1.14–1.7 litres) water to soften them enough to crush.) Add the prepared banana 'gravy' and 3 pints (1.7 litres) boiling water if the fruit has not been cooked already. Cover, cool, and add sulphite and pectin destroying enzyme. Leave covered 24 hours then add all other ingredients, mix well, take an S.G. reading and subtract from 1.131. Ferment as usual, making S.S.S. additions as necessary, finishing with an S.G. of 1.004.–1.010

ROSEHIP (2)
Wine style—Sweet social wine
3 lb. (1.36 kilos) rosehips
½ lb. (227 gm.) raisins or sultanas
2 lb. (0.9 kilo) sugar as S.S.S.
3 mg. vitamin B tablet
Pectin destroying enzyme
1 Campden tablet or 5 ml. strong sulphite solution
All purpose or Tokay yeast starter
Yeast nutrient
Water to make up the volume to 7 pints (4 litres)

Method

Prepare the rosehips as described in the previous recipe. Add the minced or liquidised dried fruit to the rosehips in a clean bucket, and pour over 3 pints (1.7 litres) boiling water if the fruit has not already been cooked. Cover, cool and add sulphite and pectin destroying enzyme. Leave covered 24 hours, then add all other ingredients, mix well, taken an S.G. reading and subtract from 1.148. Ferment as usual, making S.S.S. additions as necessary, finishing with an S.G. of 1.020.

ROSEHIP (3)

Wine style—Medium sweet social wine

By courtesy of Mr. T. D. Hodkinson—Tynemouth Winemaking Society

2¼ lb. (1.02 kilos) fresh rosehips
2 lb. (0.9 kilo) cooking apples
4 oz. (113 gm.) dried figs
2 lb. (0.9 kilo) sugar as S.S.S.
3 mg. vitamin B tablet
1 tsp. citric acid
Pectin destroying enzyme
1 Campden tablet or 5 ml. strong sulphite solution
Finely grated peel of 2 oranges
All purpose or Tokay yeast starter
Yeast nutrient
¼ teaspoonful Epsom salts
Water to make up the volume to 7 pints (4 litres)

Method

Wash the figs under running water to remove surface deposit then mince or chop into small pieces and put into a clean sterile bowl with ¼ teaspoonful Epsom salts, a pinch of yeast nutrient and ½ pint (284 ml.) water. Add the yeast starter, stir and cover, standing in a warm place. Wash the rosehips, cut and put into a sterile bucket. Wash the apples, core and chop and add to the bucket with 1 teaspoonsful nutrient. Add 2 lb. (0.9 kilo) sugar and 1 teaspoonful citric acid. Pour over 5 pints (2.84 litres) boiling water, stir to dissolve the sugar, cover and allow to cool. Add the vitamin B tablet, the pectin destroying enzyme and chopped figs which should now be in fine ferment. Ferment on the pulp for three days and strain into a sterile demijohn—allow to drain naturally. Check the S.G. and if below 1.010 add ½ lb. (227 gm.) sugar and top up to 6½ pints (3.69 litres) if necessary. When fermentation slows down, check S.G., if below 1.005, add ½ lb. sugar in syrup form. Add a further ¼ lb. (113 gm.) sugar in syrup form if the S.G. falls below 1.010 again. The final S.G. should be approximately 1.015. When fermentation ceases, rack and sulphite with 1 Campden tablet and then again at two monthly intervals. Bottle when clear.

ROSE PETAL (1)
Wine style—Dry table wine
A rosé wine may be produced by utilising red rose petals

4 pints (2.27 litres) scented rose petals
½ lb. (227 gm.) sultanas
1¾ lb. (794 gm.) sugar as S.S.S.
2, 3 mg. vitamin B tablets
Pectin destroying enzyme
1 Campden tablet or 5 ml. strong sulphite solution
2 lemons
½ cup tea or 1/30 oz. (1 gm.) grape tannin
All purpose or Bordeaux yeast starter
Yeast nutrient
Yeast energiser
Water to make up the volume to 7 pints (4 pints)

Method

Use Method 1, Chapter VI.

Place the rose petals, the juice and finely grated peel of the lemons, and the minced or liquidised sultanas in a clean bucket and pour over 2 pints (1.14 litres) boiling water. Cover, cool and add pectin destroying enzyme. Leave covered 24 hours then add all other ingredients, mix well, take an S.G. reading and subtract from 1.097 or 1.114. Ferment as usual, making S.S.S. additions as necessary, finishing with an S.G. of 0.990–1.000.

ROSE PETAL (2)
Wine style—Medium table or social wine
The use of red petals will produce a rosé wine.

4 pints (2.27 litres) scented rose petals
¾ lb. (340 gm.) currants
1¾ lb. (794 gm.) sugar as S.S.S.
2, 3 mg. vitamin B tablets
Pectin destroying enzyme
1 Campden tablet or 5 ml. strong sulphite solution
½ cup tea or 1/30 oz. (1 gm.) grape tannin
2 lemons
1 orange
All purpose or Bordeaux yeast starter
Yeast nutrient
Yeast energiser
Water to make up the volume to 7 pints (4 litres)

Method

Use Method 1, Chapter VI.

Prepare as in previous recipe, adding the juice and finely grated peel of the citrus fruit, subtracting the S.G. from 1.114.

Ferment as usual, making S.S.S. additions as necessary, finishing with an S.G. of 1.004–1.010.

ROSE PETAL (3)
Wine style—Sweet social wine

2 oz. (57 gm.) dried rose petals
(or 4 pints (2.27 litres) fresh)
¼ lb. (113 gm.) muscatel raisins
¼ lb. (113 gm.) sultanas
2¼ lb. (1.02 kilos) sugar as S.S.S.
½ cup tea or 1/30 oz. (1 gm.) grape tannin
½ oz. (14 gm.) citric or acid mixture
2, 3 mg. vitamin B tablets
Pectin destroying enzyme
1 Campden tablet or 5 ml. strong sulphite solution
All purpose or Sauternes yeast starter
Yeast nutrient
Yeast energiser
Water to make up the volume to 7 pints (4 litres)

Method

Use Method 1, Chapter VI.

Prepare the must as in Rose petal (1), subtracting the S.G from 1.148. Ferment as usual, making S.S.S. additions as necessary, finishing with an S.G. of 1.020.

SHERRIES
See Currant and Date recipes for sherries also.

DRY FINO TYPE
By courtesy of Mr. T. D. Hodkinson—Tynemouth Winemaking Society.

3 lb. (1.36 kilos) eating apples
1 lb. (454 gm.) peeled bananas
¾ pint (426 ml.) white grape concentrate
1½ lb. (680 gm.) sugar as S.S.S.
3 mg. vitamin B tablet
Pectin destroying enzyme
¼ oz. (7 gm.) cream of tartar
¼ oz. (7 gm.) Gypsom
Sherry yeast starter
Yeast nutrient
1 Campden tablet or 5 ml. strong sulphite solution
Water to make up the voume to 7 pints (4 litres)

Method

Mince and press the juice from the apples, sulphiting the juice in the receiving vessel. Prepare the banana 'gravy' and

197

add to the apple juice in a sterilised demijohn. Add all other ingredients and cover the neck of the jar with a tissue or plug with cotton wool for a few days before replacing with an air-lock. Ferment out to 0.990. Leave to settle until clear, then rack carefully into a clean polythene 1 gallon (4.5 litres) container leaving the vessel only $\frac{5}{6}$ full. *Do not sulphite*. Plug the neck of the container with cotton wool and leave for a few months until oxidation produces the fino sherry character, then bottle. If matured in glass, the oxidation process takes many months longer.

AMONTILLADO TYPE

(Medium)

4 lb. (1.8 kilos) cooking apples
1 lb. (454 gm.) raisins
1 lb. (454 gm.) sugar as S.S.S.
2, 3 mg. vitamin B tablets
Sherry yeast starter
Pectin destroying enzyme
1 Campden tablet or 5 ml. strong sulphite solution
Yeast nutrient
Water to make up the volume to 7 pints (4 litres)

Method

Use Method 2, Chapter VI.

Wash and chop the apples and put them immediately into a sterilised bucket containing 3 pints (1.7 litres) *cold* water to which the sulphite has been added (to prevent oxidative browning). Add the minced or liquidised raisins and pectin destroying enzyme and leave covered 24 hours. Next day, add all other ingredients, mix well and take an S.G. reading—subtract from 1.148. Ferment as usual, making S.S.S. additions as necessary, finishing with an S.G. of 1.006–1.010. When all the S.S.S. has been added and the required final S.G. has been obtained, leave to settle until clear, then rack into a clean 1 gallon (4.5 litres) polythene container, leaving the vessel $\frac{5}{6}$ full. *Do not sulphite*. Plug the neck of the vessel with cotton wool. Rack a second time only if another heavy sediment is thrown down. Leave to mature for a few months to a year until the true sherry-like character has developed, then bottle.

OLOROSO SHERRY TYPE (1)

Won V.H.C.—Sweet sherry class—N.Y. & S.D. Show 1976.

    1 lb. (454 gm.) wheat
    2 lb. (0.9) kilo) raisins
    1½ lb. (680 gm.) brown sugar as S.S.S.
    2 large potatoes
    2, 3 mg. vitamin B tablets
    Pectin destroying enzyme
    1 Campden tablet or 5 ml. strong sulphite solution
    Sherry yeast starter
    Yeast nutrient
    Water to make up the volume to 7 pints (4 litres)

Method

Wash and drain the wheat, then put it in a clean bowl and cover with ½–1 pint (284 ml.–568 ml.) boiling water—leave over-night. Next day mince or liquidise the wheat and the raisins and put them into a sterilised bucket. Add the potatoes, peeled and finely sliced and pour over 3 pints (1.7 litres) boiling water. Cover, cool and add sulphite and pectin destroying enzyme. Leave covered 24 hours then add all other ingredients, mix well, take an S.G. reading and subtract from 1.148. Ferment as usual, making S.S.S. additions as necessary finishing with an S.G. of 1.020. Mature as described in the previous recipe.

OLOROSO SHERRY TYPE (2)

By courtesy of Mr. R. Jackson—Tynemouth Winemaking Society.
This wine won V.H.C.—Sweet aperitif class—N.Y. & S.D. Show 1976

    1 lb. (454 gm.) raisins
    1 lb. (454 gm.) white grapes
    ½ lb. (227 gm.) dates
    3 medium potatoes
    1½ lb. (680 gm.) brown or Demerara sugar as S.S.S.
    2, 3 mg. vitamin B tablets
    Pectin destroying enzyme
    1 Campden tablet or 5 ml. strong sulphite solution
    Sherry yeast starter
    Yeast nutrient
    Water to make up the volume to 7 pints (4 litres)

Method

Use Method 1, Chapter VI

Crush the grapes in a sterilised bucket and add the minced or liquidised raisins, chopped and stoned dates and peeled, sliced potatoes. Pour over 3 pints (1.7 litres) boiling water, cover, cool and add sulphite and pectin destroying enzyme. Leave covered 24 hours, then add all other ingredients, mix well, take an S.G. reading and subtract from 1.148. Ferment as usual, making S.S.S. additions as necessary, finishing with an S.G. of 1.020. Mature as described in the first sherry recipe.

<h1 align="center">SLOE</h1>
Wine style—Medium social wine

3 lb. (1.36 kilos) sloes
2 lb. (0.9 kilo) sugar as S.S.S.
3 mg. vitamin B tablet
1 Campden tablet or 5 ml. strong sulphite solution
All purpose yeast starter
Yeast nutrient
Water to make up the volume to 7 pints (4 litres)

Method

Use Method 1, Chapter VI.

Crush the sloes by hand (wear rubber gloves) and place in a sterilised bucket. Pour over 3 pints (1.7 litres) of boiling water. Cover, cool and add sulphite and pectin destroying enzyme. Leave covered 24 hours then add all other ingredients, mix well, take an S.G. reading and subtract from 1.131. Ferment as usual, making S.S.S. additions as necessary, finishing with an S.G. of 1.006–1.014.

<h1 align="center">STRAWBERRY (1)</h1>
Wine style—Medium social wine

3 lb. (1.36 kilos) strawberries
2¼ lb. (1.02 kilos) sugar as S.S.S.
½ lb. (227 gm.) sultanas
3 mg. vitamin B tablet
Pectin destroying enzyme
1 Campden tablet or 5 ml. strong sulphite solution
½ cup tea or 1/30 oz. (1 gm.) grape tannin
All purpose or Tokay yeast starter
Yeast nutrient
Water to make up the volume to 7 pints (4 litres)

Method

Use Method 1, Chapter VI.

Wash the strawberries and crush them in a sterilised bucket. Add the minced or liquidised sultanas and 2½ pints (1.42 litres) boiling water. Cover, cool and add sulphite and pectin destroying enzyme. Leave covered 24 hours, then add all other ingredients, mix well, take an S.G. reading and subtract from 1.131. Ferment as usual, making S.S.S. additions as necessary, finishing with an S.G. of 1.006–1.014. The colour of this wine is a pleasing deep rosé.

STRAWBERRY (2)
Wine style—Sweet social wine

1½ bottles Quosh strawberry cordial
1¼ lb. (567 gm.) sugar as S.S.S.
½ pint (284 ml.) white or red grape concentrate
1 cup tea or 1/15 oz. (2 gm.) grape tannin
3 mg. vitamin B tablet
Pectin destroying enzyme
All purpose or Tokay yeast starter
Yeast nutrient
Yeast energiser
Water to make up the volume to 7 pints (4 litres)

Method

Compare Method 3, Chapter VI.

Simmer the cordial for 3 minutes to remove excess preservative. When cool, pour it into a clean demijohn and add all other ingredients, mix well, take an S.G. reading and subtract from 1.148. Ferment as usual, making S.S.S. additions as necessary, finishing with an S.G. of 1.020.

STRAWBERRY (3)
Wine style—Sweet social wine

3 lb. (1.36 kilos) strawberries
½ lb. (227 gm.) raisins
1 lb. (454 gm.) peeled over-ripe bananas
2 lb. (0.9 kilo) sugar as S.S.S.
3 mg. vitamin B tablet
Pectin destroying enzyme
½ cup tea or 1/30 oz. (1 gm.) grape tannin
1 Campden tablet or 5 ml. strong sulphite solution
All purpose or Tokay yeast starter
Yeast nutrient
Water to make up the volume to 7 pints (4 litres)

Method

Wash the strawberries and crush in a sterilised bucket. Add the minced or liquidised raisins and the prepared banana 'gravy'. Pour over 2½ pints (1.42 litres) boiling water cover, cool and add sulphite and pectin destroying enzyme. Leave 24 hours then add all other ingredients, mix well, take an S.G. reading and subtract from 1.148. Ferment as usual, making S.S.S. additions as necessary, finishing with an S.G of 1.020.

SULTANA (1)
Wine style—Medium social wine

1lb (454 gm.) sultanas
1¾ lb. (794 gm.) sugar as S.S.S.
¼ oz. (7 gm.) citric or mixed acids
Pectin destroying enzyme
3 mg. vitamin B tablet
All purpose yeast starter
Yeast nutrient
Water to make up the volume to 7 pints (4 litres)

Method

Use Method 3, Chapter VI.

Mince or liquidise the sultanas and put them in a nylon straining bag tied around the top. Cook in a pan in 3 pints (1.7 litres) water for 45 minutes to 1 hour *or* pressure cook for 15–20 minutes at 15 lbs. (6.8 kilos.) pressure, in 1 pint (568 ml.) water. After cooking, hang up the straining bag to drain. When cool, measure the amount of liquor and pour into a clean demijohn, and add all other ingredients, mix well, take an S.G. reading and subtract from 1.131. Ferment as usual, making S.S.S. additions as necessary, finishing with an S.G. of 1.006–1.014.

SULTANA (2)
Wine style—Sweet social wine

1 lb. (454 gm.) sultanas
1 bottle Quosh grapefruit and pineapple cordial
1¾ lb. (794 gm.) sugar as S.S.S.
2, 3 mg. vitamin B tablets
1 Campden tablet or 5 ml. strong sulphite solution
Pectin destroying enzyme
All purpose yeast starter
Yeast nutrient
Water to make up the volume to 7 pints (4 litres)

Method

Use Method 1, Chapter VI.

Mince or liquidise the sultanas and place in a sterilised bucket. Pour over 2 pints (1.14 litres) boiling water. Simmer the cordial for 3 minutes to remove excess preservative, then add it to the sultanas. Cover, cool and add sulphite and pectin destroying enzyme. Leave covered 24 hours then add all other ingredients, mix well, take an S.G. reading and subtract from 1.148. Ferment as usual, making S.S.S. additions as necessary, finishing with an S.G. of 1.020.

SULTANA (3)

Wine style—Sweet social or Sauternes type wine

1 lb. (454 gm.) sultanas

4 medium oranges

2 lb. (0.9 kilo) sugar as S.S.S.

3 mg. vitamin B tablet

Pectin destroying enzyme

All purpose or Sauternes yeast starter

Yeast nutrient

Yeast energiser

Water to make up the volume to 7 pints (4 litres)

Method

Use Method 3, Chapter VI.

Finely grate the peel of the oranges, pour over $\frac{1}{2}$ pint (284 ml.) boiling water and leave to infuse 24 hours. Next day cook the sultanas as in Sultana (1). Measure the amount of liquor obtained when cool and pour into a sterilised demijohn. Squeeze the juice from the oranges, strain and add it and all other ingredients to the sultana liquor, straining the orange peel infusion and adding the liquor to the demijohn. Mix well, take an S.G. reading and subtract from 1.148. Ferment as usual, making S.S.S. additions as necessary, finishing with an S.G. of 1.020.

WHEAT

(See Sherry section)

YARROW

Wine style—Medium social wine

3 pints (1.7 litres) yarrow florets
½ lb. (227 gm.) sultanas
2 lb. (0.9 kilo) sugar as S.S.S.
2, 3 mg. vitamin B tablets
Pectin destroying enzyme
¼ oz. (7 gm.) citric or mixed acids
2 oranges
½ cup tea or 1/30 oz. (1 gm.) grape tannin
All purpose yeast starter
Yeast nutrient
1 Campden tablet or 5 ml. strong sulphite solution
Yeast energiser
Water to make up the volume to 7 pints (4 litres)

Method

Use Method 1, Chapter VI.

Put the flower heads and the juice and finely grated peel of the oranges into a clean bucket. Pour over 2 pints (1.14 litres) boiling water and add the minced or liquidised sultanas. Cover, cool and add sulphite and pectin destroying enzyme. Leave covered 24 hours then add all other ingredients, mix well, take an S.G. reading and subtract from 1.131. Ferment as usual, making S.S.S. additions as necessary, finishing with an S.G. of 1.006–1.014.

LIQUEURS

For those who wish to produce liqueurs which closely resemble their commercial counterparts, Ren Bellis's book, *Making Inexpensive Liqueurs* is most useful. Here we will only concern ourselves with the simple, basic technique of liqueur making, with a few sample recipes. The proportions of ingredients in the recipes may be altered to suit one's own tastes.

The main requirement is Polish spirit or 140° proof Vodka, which may be obtained from off-licences. Even a half bottle is very expensive, but when one considers that it can be utilised to make 3 or 4 half bottles of liqueur, the expense can be seen to be worthwhile. If one holidays abroad, one should be able to acquire 100° proof Vodka very cheaply! This is the next best thing to Polish spirit since only a little more spirit of 100° proof is required. Generally speaking, the strongest Vodka available in this country is 80° proof.

Next in importance is the choice of liqueur flavourings. Some brands are of inferior quality as I have found to my cost in the past. T. Noirot produce an excellent range to suit all tastes and they may be used with confidence.

Each recipe is for a half bottle (13 fl. oz. or 370 ml.) of liqueur. They may be consumed immediately, but do improve with keeping for a few weeks or months.

CHERRY BRANDY TYPE

2nd Prize—Liqueur class—N.W. Federation Show—1976 and
3rd Prize N.Y. & S.D. Show 1977
    3–4 fl. oz. (85–114 ml.) 140° proof Polish spirit
    5 fl. oz. (142 ml.) sugar syrup
    1 tablespoonful glycerine
    1–2 large teaspoonful T. Noirot Cherry Brandy extract
    Dessert elderberry or cherry wine

Mix the spirit, sugar syrup and glycerine in a glass or plastic measuring jug and top up to 13 fl. oz. (370 ml.) with the wine. Add the liqueur extract to taste, mixing thoroughly.

APRICOT OR PEACH BRANDY TYPE

    3–4 fl. oz. (85–114 ml.) 140° proof Polish spirit
    5 fl. oz. (85–114 ml.) sugar syrup
    1 tablespoonful glycerine
1–2 large teaspoonsful T. Noirot Apricot or Peach Brandy extract
    Dessert apricot or peach wine (banana is a good substitute)

Mix together as for Cherry Brandy.

CURACAO TYPE

(1) 3–4 fl. oz. (85–114 ml.) 140° proof Polish spirit
    5 fl. oz. (142 ml.) sugar syrup
    1 tablespoonful glycerine
    1–2 large tablespoonsful T. Noirot Curacao extract
    Dessert orange wine

Mix as in the Cherry Brandy recipe.

(2) Peel of 1 orange
    5–6 fl. oz. (142–170 ml.) 140° proof Polish spirit
    5 fl. oz. (142 ml.) sugar syrup
    1 tablespoonful glycerine
    1–2 large teaspoonsful T. Noirot Curacao extract
    Orange wine

Soak the finely grated peel of the orange in the spirit overnight. Strain and mix the liquor with all other ingredients.

GREEN CHARTREUSE TYPE

6 fl. oz. (170 ml.) 140° proof Polish spirit
5 fl. oz. (142 ml.) sugar syrup
1 tablespoonful glycerine
1–2 large teaspoonsful T. Noirot Green Convent extract
Strong white wine

Mix together as in the Cherry Brandy recipe.

CREME DE MENTHE TYPE

3–4 fl. oz. (85–114 ml.) 140° proof Polish spirit
5 fl. oz. (142 ml.) sugar syrup
1 tablespoonful glycerine
1–2 teaspoonsful T. Noirot Green Mint extract
White wine

Mix together as in Cherry Brandy recipe.

ADVOCAAT

6 eggs
1 large tin Nestles condensed milk
6 drops vanilla essence
25 fl. oz. (710 ml.) sweet wine
2 measures brandy
Yellow colouring

Separate the yolks from the whites and use the yolks only. Whisk for 6 minutes. Add the condensed milk and whisk for a further 6 minutes, then add the essence, a few drops of yellow colouring and brandy and slowly fold in the wine. Store in a well stoppered bottle, preferably in a refrigerator.

SLOE GIN

Fill a 2 lb. (0.9 kilo) jam jar with well pricked sloes. Add sugar at the rate of 8–10 oz. (227–283 gm.) sugar per pound of sloes. Cover the fruit with gin and seal the jar. Agitate daily for 2–3 months then strain through a fine mesh straining bag and bottle.

INDEX